OUTSIDE
THE SUBJECT

Translated by
Michael B. Smith

Stanford
University
Press

Stanford
California
1994

OUTSIDE
THE SUBJECT

Emmanuel Levinas

Stanford University Press
Stanford, California

© Editions Fata Morgana 1987

English translation © 1993 The Athlone Press

First published in France in 1987 as *Hors Sujet*
by Fata Morgana, Saint Clement
Originating publisher of English edition
The Athlone Press, London

First published in the U.S.A. by
Stanford University Press

Printed in Great Britain

Cloth ISBN 0-8047-2197-1
Paper ISBN 0-8047-2199-8
Original printing 1993

∞ This book is printed on acid-free paper.

Original printing 1993

Last figure below indicates year of this printing:
04 03 02 01 00 99 98 97 96 95

To the memory of
Jean Nordmann
faithful to the One,
present to others

Contents

Contents

Acknowledgments

The translator wishes to express his gratitude to Jenny Overton, for her alert and intelligent text editing, to Kathy Gann, whose professional services in manuscript preparation were made available to him by Berry College, to previous translators of several of the essays contained in this volume whose work he had the benefit of consulting (see "Bibliographical Information"), and to his wife Helen for her unfailing encouragement.

Bibliographical Information

"Martin Buber's Thought and Contemporary Judaism" is the text of a lecture, published in the collection *Martin Buber. L'homme et le philosophe* (Brussels: Editions de l'Institut de Sociologie de l'Université Libre de Bruxelles, 1968).

"Martin Buber, Gabriel Marcel and Philosophy" is the text of a paper delivered at the Buber Centenary Conference held at the Ben Gurion University of the Negev in January, 1978. It was published in *Revue Internationale de Philosophie* (126 [1978]); and in English in *Martin Buber. A Centenary Volume*, ed. J. Bloch and H. Gordon, trans. E. Kameron (New York: Ktav Publishing House, 1984).

"Apropos of Buber: Some Notes" appeared in the collection *Qu'est-ce que l'homme? Philosophie/Psychanalyse. Hommage à Alphonse de Waelhens (1911–1981)* (Brussels: Facultés Universitaires Saint-Louis, 1982).

"Franz Rosenzweig: A Modern Jewish Thinker" appeared in *Revue de Théologie et de Philosophie* (98 [1965]).

"Jean Wahl: Neither Having nor Being" appeared in the collection *Jean Wahl et Gabriel Marcel*, ed. Jeanne Hersch (Paris: Beauchesne, 1976).

"Vladimir Jankélévitch" was published in *L'Information juive* (July, 1985).

"The Meaning of Meaning" appeared in *Heidegger et la question de Dieu*, ed. R. Kearney and J. S. O'Leary (Paris: Grasset & Fasquelle, 1980).

"On Intersubjectivity: Notes on Merleau-Ponty" appeared in the collection *Paradigmes de théologie philosophique. En hommage à Marie-Dominique Philippe, O. P.*, ed. O. Hoeffe and R. Imbach (Fribourg: Editions Universitaires, 1983); and in English, in *Ontology and Alterity in Merleau-Ponty*, trans. M. B. Smith (Evanston: Northwestern University Press, 1990).

"In Memory of Alphonse de Waelhens" appeared in *Tijdschrift voor Filosofie* (46 [1984]). The section headed "On Sensibility" also appeared in English in *Ontology and Alterity in Merleau-Ponty*, op. cit.

"The Rights of Man and the Rights of the Other" appeared in the collection *L'indivisibilité des droits de l'homme* (Fribourg: Editions Universitaires, 1985).

"The Strings and the Wood: On the Jewish Reading of the Bible" appeared in the May–June special issue of *Axes* (4 [1972]).

"Everyday Language and Rhetoric without Eloquence" appeared in *Le quotidien et la philosophie, Philosophica*, vol. 40 (Bern/Stuttgart: Verlag Paul Haupt, 1981).

"The Transcendence of Words: On Michel Leiris's *Biffures*" appeared in *Les Temps Modernes* (44 [1949]).

"Outside the Subject" was written especially for this volume.

Translator's Introduction

The author himself has furnished a preface to this volume, summarizing its content and even undertaking, in very condensed form, to specify its relationship to "the overall inquiry of which these studies are but moments." It is true that his preface does not mention two short pieces, "The Meaning of Meaning," which challenges the Heideggerian derivation of all meaning from Being, and "The Strings and the Wood," on the relationship between text and tradition in the Jewish reading of the Bible; but otherwise Levinas's own account requires little supplement.

The French would refer to this volume as a *"recueil"* rather than as a *"collection"* or an *"anthologie."* The first term designates a work assembled by the author: part of the meaning of the work is therefore to be sought in the ordering of its parts. Levinas has placed his studies devoted to other thinkers in the order of their time rather than by date of composition, as would an editor of a compilation of Levinas's texts. Such an editor might also note that the texts were written over a span of almost forty years (1949–87), and that they are bound together by a preface and a concluding essay, written especially for this volume, whose role it is to provide closure for the rest.

These two "binding" pieces, because of their ambition of explicating the volume's unifying principle and setting it in

relation to the whole of Levinas's ethical philosophy, paradoxically present the most difficulties of interpretation (as they
have of translation); therefore I shall offer my own explicative
reading of them. But before that I shall supply some information
on the general relationship between Levinas's thought and that
of three figures who have influenced him greatly and are
eminently present in the pages of *Outside the Subject*: Edmund
Husserl (1859–1938), Martin Buber (1878–1965), and Franz
Rosenzweig (1886–1929).

Edmund Husserl

"It is undoubtedly Husserl who is at the origin of my
writings," Levinas writes in 1983.[1]

Levinas was Husserl's (and Heidegger's) student for a short
time in Freiburg. His first book (*The Theory of Intuition in
Husserl's Phenomenology*, 1930) already presents a reading of
Husserl in which future Levinasian themes can be observed. For
example, Levinas stresses the importance of Husserl's "affirmation of the intentional character of practical and axiological life"
in the concluding sentence of the above-mentioned work, and
again (fifty-seven years later!) at the end of *Outside the Subject*
(see below, p. 157): "Husserl's magnificent discovery of affective
and axiological intentionality." The "axiological" element in
Husserlian intentionality is a stepping stone on the way to the
"ethical intrigue" underlying consciousness itself in Levinas's
philosophy.

Jacques Colette's 1984 study, "Lévinas et la phénoménologie
husserlienne,"[2] astutely observes that Levinas moves from "some
reticences" in his first book on Husserl to an "increasingly
precise" opposition that, though not vanishing completely, gives
way in the later writings to "a desire to emphasize a proximity
that was undetectable in the first book." This tendency is
particularly well illustrated in the essay "Outside the Subject,"

which presents the Husserlian transcendental Ego in a surprisingly positive fashion, in light of his earlier stringent critiques. Ultimately Levinas views Husserl's phenomenology as a culmination of the entire Western tradition of philosophical reflection, a tradition that has been "a destruction of Transcendence." All notions of transcendence within the Western epistemological tradition of return (a movement of intentionality originating within the subject, perceiving a transcendence and then returning to the self in which the accumulated knowledge of experience is stored) are fated to fall back into immanence. The intersubjective relation is particularly important in Levinas's critique of Husserlian intentional analysis, since intentional consciousness seems most insufficient in accounting for it. Levinas builds his ethical relation precisely on this "intentionality that fails."[3] Further accounts of the evolution of Levinas's critique of Husserl are to be found in André Orianne's foreword to his translation of Levinas's 1930 work, *The Theory of Intuition in Husserl's Phenomenology*[4] (specifically on the problematic nature of Husserl's foundation of the reduction, and his understanding of the nature of sensation) and in Richard A. Cohen's essay, "Levinas, Rosenzweig, and the Phenomenologies of Husserl and Heidegger"[5] (showing how Levinas's readings of Heidegger and Rosenzweig oriented his critique of Husserl).

While Husserl's thematization of consciousness and the Ego is taken up by Levinas, the latter's sustained scrutiny of those themes over half a century transforms them radically. Consciousness, based on presence and/or representation, gives way to a vigilance not directed toward being, a relationship of non-aesthesiological awareness. But the characterization of this new relationship is not restricted to a string of negatives. In fact, Husserl's "appresentation" (Husserl's term for indirect perception via a direct presentation, such as that of minds through bodies) of human and cultural meaning is expressly criticized as being the negative aspect of a not-yet-articulated positivity.[6]

Husserl's phenomenology was a *sine qua non* for Levinas's own metaethics, though clearly not a *ne plus ultra*. Levinas's ipseity, as Marc Richir points out, is not only less active than Husserl's (whose "Ich" is the source of constituting consciousness), but (in Levinas's own words) "more passive than all passivity."[7] Levinas associates self with "the same," but then places otherness at the very heart of it, so that the self is a continuous awakening, a being troubled by the other, an "uncondition" or non-state. Vigilance is to consciousness as insomnia to sleep. Pinnacle of awareness, this self has no identity other than the shedding of its identity.

Although there is no specific essay devoted to Husserl in this collection, his work is present in the two pieces on Merleau-Ponty ("On Intersubjectivity" and, within Chapter 9, "On Sensibility") as well as in Levinas's preface and his last essay, "Outside the Subject," to which I shall return.

Martin Buber

Outside the Subject contains more text on Martin Buber (interspersed with some commentary on Gabriel Marcel) than any other figure. The first three pieces are devoted to him, and placed in their order of publication: 1968, 1978 and 1982. The first piece, a lecture (following a lecture given by Gabriel Marcel to the same audience–there are several allusions to it), begins with an overview of the situation of Judaism in the modern world, and then turns to Hasidism, specifically as interpreted by Buber. (It should be said in passing that Levinas is wary of the mystic tendencies of Hasidism.) Buber's interpretation is in fact a rather personal one, and may reflect some Bergsonian influence. Then Buber's biblical exegeses and translations are examined, before attention is focused on his most important theme: the I–Thou relation and the Meeting. Levinas draws the I–Thou relation into his own problematic by redescribing it as a particular instance of "presence" not determined by consciousness. He then goes a step further, introducing his own term, proximity, and suggesting that this reflection ruptures the sphere of immanence. Ultimately both the terms absence and presence are to be rejected, for they lead us back, through thematization and objectification, to ontology. The communication closes by opening onto a non-place that is "beyond being."

The second lecture on Buber is longer and more intensely focused on circumscribing the significance of the philosophy of dialogue, by establishing the commonality of the interhuman relation in both Buber and Gabriel Marcel. The latter, a Christian existentialist, is more committed to an ontology of presence than Buber: hence it seems more anomalous that the latter's "I–Thou" philosophy should remain attached to the language of presence. Levinas examines the implications of Marcel's ontological interpretation of the lived body and the principle of incarnation, and concludes that it leads to founding dialogue upon a "participation," an "intersubjective nexus" that is the vital original from which language as we know it has, by alienation, been torn away.

Beyond the differences between Buber and Marcel, Levinas heralds in their philosophy of dialogue a momentous departure from a hitherto dominant "metaphysics of the object." The third part of this piece asks a question so sweeping as to make the reader wonder whether it is merely a rhetorical device: How does dialogue respond to the very vocation of philosophy? The question is quickly given greater focus by defining what the vocation of philosophy *was*. It was the ability to say *I*, to think fully and freely (freed of *doxa* and dogma) while doing so: the ability to say *cogito*. Knowledge is adequation with being. Levinas shows the difficulties this understanding of philosophy's vocation has run into: that is, the problems inherent in identifying "meaning and intelligibility with the intellectual act of knowing." The next phase of the question is: Does the philosophy of dialogue of Buber and Marcel, which ensures the alterity of the other in a transcendence of the "Thou," correspond to philosophy's vocation? The fourth and last part attempts to answer that question (of the adequacy of dialogue) by taking up the question of language, which is after all the medium of dialogue. Here the distinction between the Saying and the Said, which plays so vital a role in Levinas's main philosophical work, *Otherwise than Being or Beyond Essence*, first published in 1974, four years prior to this piece. The Saying is associated with the more fluent aspect of language, while the Said reflects its thematizing modality. More specifically, it appears that the realm of the Said falls under the sway of the "I–It" relation, since things said are intended as objects, while the Saying is essentially dialogical and "vocative." In conclusion, and as we have now come to anticipate (for this is the movement of so many of Levinas's discussions of other philosophers' work), Levinas moves beyond Buber into his own speculative domain: a space of "neither representation nor knowledge nor ontology." An "ethics of heteronomy" that offers "a new way of understanding the possibility of an I," an identity by uniqueness vis-à-vis the other. In the final pages there is a sudden emergence of quotations from Husserl, who represents the ultimate confines of the European tradition of metaphysics understood as the project of turning experience into knowledge. And Husserl himself, in this *Lebenswelt* phase, shows an awareness of the sea in which theoretical reflection is afloat; but he sees it, according to Levinas, as but "an interruption of pure concession to the weakness of our non-angelic natures." The concluding paragraph is a talmudic quotation, which takes up the epithet "angelic." If the Torah was given to mankind (and not to the angels) it was because men die and eat and buy and sell. Their potential for being-for-one-another places them "above and beyond the understanding of the being to which pure spirits are consigned."

The third piece on Buber ("Apropos of Buber: Some Notes") focuses on Levinas's own departures from the Buber–Marcel version of the dialogue in a more succinct and penetrating manner. First, there is a rapid synopsis of Buber's achievement in ontological terms. The otherness of the other is a far more impregnable transcendence than that of things in the "outer world," which we do somehow interiorize in knowledge. Hence the epistemological ambiguity of immanence and transcendence is left behind. Hence also, if the "I–Thou" relation is taken seriously, the role of language is transformed from a purely ancillary one, a servant of thought in the idealist tradition, to becoming "the very bursting forth of thought dialogically coming out of itself."

Levinas's criticism of Buber's account of the "I–Thou" relation is that it is equal, symmetrical and reversible. Without the other's being "first," and above myself, there can be no ethical relation. Levinas also suggests that Buber fails to overcome the dualism between the "I–Thou" and the "I–It" relation. This would account for the ethereal atmosphere of rarified spirituality Levinas attributes to the Buberian "Meeting." Must not third-person things (such as food and shelter) already be extant for generosity to be possible?

Levinas's critique of Buber's "I–Thou" relation is perhaps most succinctly formulated in five questions put directly to Buber in an *Interrogation of Martin Buber* conducted by Maurice S. Friedman and published in English in 1964.[8] Already evident in the questions is the emergence of a new concept, "illeity," (derived from the Latin demonstrative "*ille*") to designate the relation of man to God, in the "trace" of which the self also encounters the other person.

The most detailed treatment of Levinas's relation to Buber is that of Robert Bernasconi, whose "'Failure of Communication' as a Surplus: Dialogue and Lack of Dialogue between Buber and Levinas"[9] uses Jacques Derrida's 1964 essay "Violence and Metaphysics"[10] as a backdrop for a careful analysis of the evolution of Levinas's reading of Buber, using virtually all of Levinas's numerous studies on Buber, but also working closely enough with the texts of Buber to avoid a simple rehearsal of the Levinasian reading of the latter. Bernasconi concludes that their relationship, though not culminating in agreement or even a clear understanding of one another's differences, was an instancing of that "restlessness of the same disturbed by the other" of which Levinas speaks in *Otherwise than Being or Beyond Essence.*[11]

Franz Rosenzweig

Levinas wrote three accounts of Franz Rosenzweig's career and major work, *The Star of Redemption*. The one contained in this volume, "Franz Rosenzweig: A Modern Jewish Thinker," (1965) takes up some of the material from an earlier lecture, "Between Two Worlds."[12] The most recent piece, a nine-page introduction to a study on Rosenzweig by Stéphane Mosès, is an exposition rather than a critical examination of Rosenzweig's major themes.[13]

In an interview with Salomon Malka, Levinas says that he simply borrowed Rosenzweig's critique of Hegel.[14] And as the title of one of his most important philosophical works, *Totality and Infinity*, indicates, it is the notion of infinity (but also of subjectivity, as in Kierkegaard) that Levinas opposes to totality. The precise ways in which the notion of infinity is assigned the role of breaking through the sphere of immanence (and knowledge, and ontology) toward a stronger form of transcendence than that which stands opposed to the perceiving self cannot be exposited more fully here. But there is another philosophical debt toward Rosenzweig to which Levinas often refers: the technique of "deformalization of the concept," specifically the rethinking of the relation between God and the world as creation (and past), the relation between God and man as revelation (and present), and that between man (already illuminated by revelation) and the (already created) world as redemption (and future). These "living" or original syntheses are assured by the connectedness of time, reflected in the "religio" (tying together) of religion.

A third aspect of Rosenzweig's importance for Levinas is his exemplary nature as a Jew who was open to the world and all the intellectual forces of his time, chose Judaism and went on thinking and writing in full philosophical and theological autonomy. He saw the existence of Judaism and Christianity (he is severe toward Islam) as philosophically necessary. J.-J. Schlegel, in describing the relationship between Levinas and Rosenzweig, and by way of explaining why the latter has not received the critical treatment others (Husserl, Heidegger, Buber) have, surmises: "he apparently represents more of a spiritual filiation, with all the delicacy and respect that goes with it, than a philosophical influence; a lived complicity more than a theoretical challenge."[15] Though it would be a mistake to minimize the strictly conceptual influence, there clearly were other affinities. Levinas speaks admiringly of Rosenzweig's decision to leave a promising academic career in order to found a Jewish Studies Center ("Freies jüdisches Lehrhaus") in Frankfurt:[16] and he himself devoted much time and energy after 1947 to participating in and encouraging Judaic studies, particularly study of the Talmud.

Levinas's Preface

Levinas has produced, in his attempt to introduce this book, a condensed and difficult synopsis. He begins by saying what the book is *not* about. The type of reflection it will engage in is not impersonal, not about an outer, objective reality. Now, that objective reality has as its supporting correlative a subjectivity, an "impassive identity" or "I." This "I" is, accordingly, termed "objectifying," or "transcendental." It, too, is evoked only to be differentiated from that which constitutes the true preoccupation of the authors whose works are to be considered here—the true subject-matter of the book. But it is important to note that Levinas is not rejecting the validity of the (Husserlian) transcendental *Ego*: this explains why he is careful to defend it, in passing, from more naive psychologistic or naturalistic concepts of the self, precisely those critiqued by Husserl. Though not rejecting Husserl's transcendental Ego, Levinas does deny its status as unconditioned origin, for he suggests that sociality and proximity "may have contributed to the very emergence of the transcendental 'I'," and goes on to speak of an "ethical genesis" of objectivity, of the realm of knowledge and truth. This ground-floor level of "spiritual intrigue" between humans is the milieu from which both subjects and objects arise. It should be observed that Levinas's term "sociality" must be kept distinct from the cultural sense it has in the social sciences.

Now Levinas broadens his consideration in order to formulate the overall orientation of his philosophy–again, by negation. It is not an attempt to deny the possibility of knowledge. The possibility of knowledge is immediately associated with the transformation of the known into some sort of object. Now, the human being risks being misunderstood and misused in this operation. The essentially human eludes this knowing. There is an order higher than that of knowledge. At this point the characteristic for which Levinas's philosophy is best known is introduced. It is the most radical departure from prior philosophers. Levinas proposes that the being that perseveres in its being (the Spinozan *"conatus essendi"* the "trying to be") is interrupted by the emergence within being of the human.

It is not a question of putting knowledge in doubt, but it is clearly a question of relativizing knowledge. In fact, much of Levinas's philosophy consists in a critique of knowledge: a critique differing from Kant's critique in several important ways. First, knowledge does not emerge more modest but more realistic in its pretensions. Knowledge is denied and something other (better) proposed in its place. Secondly, it is not all knowledge that is critiqued, but only knowledge of persons.[17] Knowledge is held by Levinas to be a kind of violence, when deployed against human beings. It comprehends, engulfs and assimilates the other into the (self)same. The other is to be encountered (*à la* Buber, by and large), addressed in dialogue.

The violence inherent in knowledge is implicated in the violence of (Heideggerian) ontology, in which knowledge is a dimension of existence, and in Husserlian phenomenology, in which being and knowing meet in the optimum of the manifestation, the "presence" of the phenomenon. This violence is embedded in existence, in being or "essence" (Levinas's term for the verbal aspect of being), in the "*conatus essendi*" alluded to above: it is present in all forms of being.

> Origin of all violence, diverse according to the diverse modes of being: the life of living beings, the existence of human beings, the reality of things. The life of the living, in the struggle for life; the natural history of humans in the blood and tears of struggle between persons, nations and classes; the matter of things, hard matter; solidity; the closed-in-upon-itself, down to the intra-atomic confinement of the physicists.[18]

These considerations are of a clearly metaphysical nature. They lead (or point) to what David Banon has called the "diptych" of Levinas's oeuvre, emphasizing the hinges, but insisting nevertheless on the distinction between the "philosophical" (or "Greek") panel and the "religious" or "Jewish" one.[19] In the text before us–the conclusion of Levinas's preface to *Outside the Subject*–the word "order" is just such a hinge. "An order higher than knowing," is repeated at the beginning of the penultimate paragraph, but now its other meaning (order as command) is intended. The dialectic of the indicative yields to the ethical "intrigue" of the vocative and the imperative.

For readers of Levinas, this movement from the reassuring, the "philosophical" (or "Greek," i.e. the dialectic founded on such concepts as subject, object, category, etc.) to a more troubling discourse in which certain terms (the "face," the "trace," a past that never was present. . .) begin to play by different rules of coherence, is well known. It is the passage toward a domain for which philosophy is doubtless not the only route.

> I have tried, above all, to see the ethical in relation to the rationality of the knowledge that is immanent to being, which rationality is primordial in the philosophical tradition of the West, even though ethics (which, after all, goes beyond the forms and determinations

of ontology, but does not for all that renounce the peace of the Reasonable) could lead to another version of intelligibility and another way of loving wisdom. And perhaps even (but I will not go that far) to the way of Psalm 111: 10.[20]

True, it is in Levinas's books of talmudic studies (e.g. his *Nine Talmudic Readings*) that this other version of intelligibility is more fully explored. But already the movement from the dialectic to the dialogical (via Buber and Marcel) suggests the possibility ("toward which" so many of Levinas's essays end, so to speak) of a Levinasian coherence–an original "neither" issued from a Greek-Judaic both. Such is the movement of the concluding eponymous essay, "Outside the Subject," which attempts to trace a path (more precisely it summarizes, in an allusive, cryptic fashion, the tracing of a path in earlier pieces written in the 1970s, most of which are collected in *De Dieu qui vient à l'idée*) from Husserl's transcendental Ego to a non-intentional, passive subjectivity, to be described in ethical terms such as "sincerity," "timidity," or "bad conscience," rather than in epistemological ones.

"Outside the Subject"

This final essay is composed of five very short parts (each containing from one to three paragraphs), titled respectively "From Subject to Object," "From Object to Subject," "The Pure Ego," "A Subject Outside the Subject," and "Before Truth." On the basis of these headings alone we may briefly describe the movement of the essay as follows. The movement from the subject to the object reflects Husserl's critique of late nineteenth-century empiricism's attempt to naturalize consciousness, reducing it to an impersonal (or third-person) status. Having made subjectivity into a special realm filled with mental objects, and the mind a domain in which natural processes and laws could be formulated to account for the products of a hitherto free and undetermined ego, psychology seemed to achieve a new unified ontological field. Husserl's *Logical Investigations* (1901) challenged this subjectification of the world of ideas by emphasizing the objective "ideas" that might be in–but were not of–consciousness. (This is Levinas's reading of Husserl's famous "Consciousness is always consciousness *of* something.") Unfortunately, however, this way of presenting the world came dangerously close to a return to precritical naive realism. Hence we move on to the next section, "From Object to Subject," to find, still within Husserl, the opposite movement: true objectivity must include the horizonal phenomena out of which the thematized object emerges. The object must not be divorced from the "intentional" subjective structure in which it arises. Objectivity is constituted, and that constituted objectivity must never be used to explain the noetic-noematic field in which it was constituted. It is precisely Husserl's *phenomenological reduction* that allows these constituting structures to emerge, prior to all ontological dogmatism, all judgment as to what "really exists." The "concrete" is not the scientific object but the phenomenon that is experienced in its own way, on its own terms.

At the heart of experience there is, in the Husserl of *Ideas* (*Ideen I*, 1913) a pure Ego, the remainder after the transcendental reduction. Levinas insists that this Ego is not an abstraction, nor impersonal: the pure I is a personal one, a unique and paradoxical "transcendence in immanence."

This pure identity now becomes (in part 4 of the essay) Levinas's focal point for further investigation. It is "different because of its uniqueness," not "unique because of its difference." That is to say, there is no inherent quality within the Ego that sets it off from all others, as might be the case with members of an existing set. Uniqueness is itself the (only) quality of the Ego: it is essentially uniqueness. It is at this point that Levinas goes beyond elucidating Husserl's thought. No doubt for both thinkers it is impossible to characterize the pure, transcendental Ego: but Levinas attempts to suggest its modality as "incessant awakening." This characterization in fact anticipates a further development, not clearly stated in this essay, but carefully worked out elsewhere, in which the self is decentered in relation to itself, and the "me" (*moi*) distinguished from the "self" (*soi*). Still, the overall role of this fourth section is to accredit Husserl with the isolation of this rarefied conception of the Ego, which the latter had described (negatively) as "indescribable pure Ego and nothing more."

The fifth and last part of the essay takes up the phrase "and nothing more" in the interrogatory mode. Perhaps there is something more. Something more than the constituting and knowing subject, something more than, and prior to, the accomplishment of knowledge, or truth. That something more and other than the Husserlian ego is characterized as being "anterior" to knowledge. But this anteriority is not that of a prior present. The manner or thinking to which this earlier, ethical subject becomes available is a non-ontological one in which there is neither noesis nor noema, and no synchronic time in which it would be possible to "re-present" dispersed temporalities into an overall "theory." Along with theory (from Greek *thea*, a viewing), the light of the *intuitus mentis* is transcended, since this uniqueness is "ordered. . .in a different light than the one illuminating the structures of the phenomenon. . ." As Catherine Chalier comments, that light, the light of "the absolute anteriority of God," who can never "give himself simply in a now," is "a light come from the deepest erstwhile of creation, an immemorial past."[21]

This is no longer the transcendental "I" in the Husserlian sense; first, because it is best referred to not as "I" but as "me," in the "accusative" case–that is, as it would be referred to by a subjectivity referring to itself from the outside; second, because this transcendence is not doomed, as any intentional object would be, to immanence, to being part of a totality. It is "otherwise than being." Though Levinas sets Husserl's texts to work in a way their author may not have foreseen, this reinterpretation of the "pure I," a discovery of the transcendental reduction, is attributed to the Husserlian "unthought." In the words of Merleau-Ponty, another great explorer of subjectivity in Husserl's wake: "At the end of Husserl's life there is an unthought-of element in his works which is wholly his yet opens out on something else."[22] The very maladroitness of the last line of this essay, doubling back as if with a fond reluctance to leave the phenomenological field, marks the recognition of indebtedness on the part of a thinker already solicited elsewhere.

A Note on this Translation

Levinas frequently writes his own translation of biblical passages from the Hebrew. Hence I have chosen to translate his French, which reflects his interpretation. But I have also consulted *The Holy Scriptures* (Philadelphia: The Jewish Publication Society of America, 1917). Verse numbers, particularly in the psalms, may vary slightly from those used in most Christian Bibles.

While I have attempted to translate into nonsexist language, I have in some cases preferred to let "man" or "men" and its consequent "his" remain, in cases where clarity would have been sacrificed or no reasonably graceful alternative could be found. The context should make it clear that women are to be thought of as included, as in earlier English usage.

Preface

In this collection the reader will find certain texts of mine–previously scattered in various publications–devoted to the works of a few contemporary philosophers who bring out and champion the thought that informs–or rather realizes and sustains–the proximity of person to person, the proximity of one's neighbor or the welcome we prepare for one another. It is a mode of thought that cannot be reduced to an act of knowing in which truths are constituted–in which this or that thing, showing itself within the consciousness of an *I*, presents or maintains its being in the objectivity or exteriority of appearance, borne by the impassive identity of this *I*. Such is the identity of the objectifying *I*, the "transcendental *I*"–an identity neither resulting from a logical operation of identification, functioning within reflection, objectifying an inner given, nor emerging into consciousness from the depths of a prior unconscious, but the identity of an *I* that from the start, without objectifying reflection, is a *self*, the identity of an *ipseity*.

That *immanence* of being, accessible to the subject in objectivity, that intelligibility of the objective in knowing, bears no resemblance to the proximity of the neighbor, the sociality that appears to interest the philosophers recalled in my studies–studies which nonetheless confer upon human alterity, in the way it is received by the person, the dignity of

1

intelligibility. An "original" rationality, to be sure, but perhaps a rationality of origin as well, conditioning that of objects to be known–at least if it may have contributed to the very emergence of the transcendental "I," that impassive identity necessary for the objectification of being in truth.

Martin Buber, Gabriel Marcel and, to a great extent, Franz Rosenzweig, discussed in this book, have insisted upon that intelligibility outside the objectifying subject–but so have Jean Wahl, Vladimir Jankélévitch, Maurice Merleau-Ponty, Alphonse de Waelhens and Michel Leiris, implicitly, in their descriptions of the human. These latter, proceeding from problems formulated differently, using different language but prompted by philosophical inspirations no less lofty, do not limit themselves to structures imposed upon thought by the subject–object correlation to understand the meaningful in man.

To the pages concerned with these thinkers I have added two short pieces, one on the problem of the rights of man, the other on the life of language, moving from the neutrality of ideas approached in their objective meaning toward their modification "in the light of the human face," to which one must return, even though in objectification the face is already scarcely recognizable. The volume ends with a previously unpublished study which examines the role of the subject, setting out from the point of view of Husserl's phenomenology. The positing of the subject, foundational to truth–its pure and impassive identity of transcendental *I*–is then developed in the direction of an ethical genesis, a spiritual intrigue woven between humans, before their metamorphosis into subjects and objects who suspend, without stopping, that intrigue of transcendence and responsibility between unique beings from which the pure *I* arises and to which it returns.

In order to give a better sense of the importance of the thematic interrelatedness of the texts gathered here, perhaps I should hazard some indication, in this preface, of the overall inquiry of which these studies are but moments. It is not a question of putting knowledge in doubt. The human being clearly allows himself to be treated as an object, and delivers himself over to knowledge in the *truth* of perception and the light of the human sciences. But, treated exclusively as an object, man is also mistreated and misconstrued. It is not that the truth would wound or be unworthy of him. But the very emergence of the human within being is the interruption of the being that perseveres in its being, along with the connotation of violence in that notion of perseverance and *conatus essendi*–the dis-interestment possible through the human, awakening thought to an order higher than knowing. We are human before being learned, and remain so after having forgotten much.

An order higher than knowing. An order that, resounding like a call, touches the human in his individuality still congealed by the generality of the genus, but already awake to the uniqueness of the *I*, a uniqueness indiscernible by logic, in responsibility for the other person, an undeniable election, bearing love in which the other, the loved one, is to the *I* unique in the world. From unique to unique, from one to the other, beyond any relatedness, the one more foreign to the other than any exteriority that already, in the objective world, renounces itself and becomes immanent–yet henceforth, the entire "logically" new, previously unheard-of bond of social proximity, the wonder of a mode of thought better than knowledge. Outside the subject.

The resounding call of a vocation above the logic that still commands the individual through the necessities of the genus and species, the awakening to a vigilance–original and ultimate–of thought in which the other, still part of an objective world in knowledge, is also outside the world. Objects outside objects: the face to whom one says "good morning" and "thee" and "thou." At least these problems were taken seriously by Gabriel Marcel and Martin Buber. The face–human nakedness that can put on a face, but is always on the verge of shedding lies and forms–weakness, demand, already begging, but also a strange authority, defenseless yet commanding, calling out to me, I who am responsible for that misery. And ordering me, identity pure and impassive, eventually at the service of the true.

1 Martin Buber's Thought and Contemporary Judaism

It is difficult, in fifty minutes, to encompass Buber's thought, and even more difficult to summarize contemporary Jewish thought, even if I omit the part that is Jewish only by the thinkers' lineage. I speak of *thought* and not *philosophy*, because the intellectual life of Judaism which has retained its Jewishness does not present itself in terms of principles, nor should it be judged on that basis. There is the exegesis of texts, the "assumption" of one's own history, as it is termed these days, the questions raised for today's Jews by the ordeal they have just passed through, their need to regroup, to find themselves again; and along with this problem all the others (which are not purely political) concerning the existence, future and defense of the State of Israel; and lastly the confrontation with the modern world–a world economically, politically and technologically transformed and in search of a new religious equilibrium. All these elements nourish Jewish thought, which is not limited to *a soul conversing with itself.* Today, as always, Jewish thought, and the immense oeuvre of Buber in which it is reflected and in which, in many cases, it was formed, brings to strictly philosophical thought (a modality of thought forced to sustain the claim that it never encounters anyone or anything it has not seen before) the rich harvest of what our friend Professor de

Waelhens called in a remarkable recent work "non-philosophical experience"; a harvest without which philosophy would be a perfectly suitable mode of thought, but with nothing to say. Before specifying Buber's contribution to the various domains of current Jewish thought (and I will consider only a few of them), something must be said of the role he played by the very stature of his personhood and talent. It was he who showed the Western world that Judaism exists as a contemporary form of life and thought. But it was also he who taught Judaism itself that it was again visibly exposed to the outside world, present *otherwise* than by the participation of its assimilated and de-Judaicized intellectuals in the spiritual life of the West. Buber was one of the rare Jewish thinkers and writers who, through a work almost totally devoted to Jewish themes, belonged with an extraordinary naturalness, spontaneity and, as actors say, "presence," to universal literature. That grace and authority, that ease were part of his physical being as well as of his writings. His thought, beginning with a meditation on Jewish sources and especially Hasidism, took on all the problems of our day. At the dawn of the twentieth century, Buber, transcending all theology and national culture, beyond all orthodoxy, addressed post-Christian Judaism which, assimilated in the Western world, had shed all the traits peculiar to it, while in Eastern Europe it still retained its own vitality and personality, but remained apart from the surrounding world that rejected it. This contemporary Judaism, by all that remained Judaic within it, was seen in the West and the East as an anachronism, a fossil, a testimony at best, and in any case an object of historical and archeological study. (And at this point I take the liberty of recalling the phrase of Rabbi Zunz, the founder of "liberal" Judaism and that famous "science" of Judaism, who used to say: "Judaism is dead, but we are going to give it a magnificent funeral.") Buber saw post-Christian Judaism as a living civilization of admirable maturity, and brought it as a full and equal partner into the Western forum. For, through Jewish civilization, he addressed only universal questions. All the studies undertaken since then by Jewish thinkers, who demand a teaching from biblical, talmudic and kabbalist sources, often rejecting Buber–that entire quest for truth and doctrine has found a new language, the tone and cadence of which were set by Buber: a language making confrontation possible. And it is undoubtedly the indelible mark left by Buber's passage that reminded the Council fathers who voted for the most recent schema (and especially the one preceding it)[1] on relations with the Jews, that that ancient wisdom has learned to speak the modern languages and is ready, if invited, for dialogue.

The revealing of Jewish spirituality to the West and to the Jews themselves began with the studies Buber, while still very young, devoted to Hasidism, a religious movement that had developed in the eighteenth century, shortly after the failure of the adventure of the false Messiah Sabbatai Zvi. This movement, in which feeling plays a considerable role, is known for its opposition to the aristocratic intellectualism of Rabbinism. Buber was not the only one to recognize the importance of this movement in the religious development of Israel.

Hebrew and Yiddish literature, the works of Peretz in particular, translate the new Hasidic sensibility in the form of attractive and very popular tales. But it was Buber who had the idea of rethinking Hasidism outside the context of the kabbalist texts that had delineated its theory, and within the perspectives of Western thought, and of seeking in Hasidic spirituality a response to the crisis of the West itself, which he had already detected before the world wars, before National Socialism. Mr. Gabriel Marcel has shown you to what extent that consciousness of a crisis was acute in Buber, who was, nonetheless, in love with the West. That crisis of the Western world seemed to him to come from a break between the world and God, which would call into question both the secular and the religious life of the men of our time.

I have often wondered what such expressions as those mean, beyond their theological or theosophical meaning. A world without God is, I think, a world in which, according to Dostoyevsky's expression, all is permitted–in which the significance of the real world is exhausted in its appearances, and in which one must be "realistic." A God without a world would be a spiritual life with no hold on the real, a life of pure escapism, a life one stops taking seriously the moment the free time allotted to it is up. The vocation of the whole man–the vocation of the pious, the just, the man granted grace–consists, according to this conception of Hasidism, in acting within the world as if God were present everywhere, even in the immediate and the sensible. It consists in serving God not just during the time of the elevation of the cult, but in all the undertakings of everyday life. The human person, the "I," *hic et nunc*, bogged down in his or her problems or cares, is a means of sanctification. Here the human *I* is the reuniting of the profane and the sacred. It is not a substance but a relationship. Man is a bridge, as Nietzsche would have it, a passage, a going beyond. One must, following that conception of Hasidism, feel in that concrete presence to the world an elevation of the world, and one must bring out the sparks from on high that are languid here below, and restore them to the original Ardor from which they have descended.

Buber sees, through the human, an exaltation of the instants of banal time. As in many modern views, man, or the I, is essentially what is stirred up by the drama of being itself in its effort to gather, repair and draw what is fallen upward toward the heights. I use Buber's own terminology to articulate the principal theme of the interpretation he gives of Hasidism.

To exist is thus to gather up the dispersion of the sacred in the profane. This is not at all the same thing as finding oneself thrown and abandoned in the absurd, as certain philosophers of existence were soon to think, and among whom we might, for other reasons, have been able to classify Buber–if there ever were such a thing as a classified philosopher.

All this is close to what Buber teaches in his general philosophy, which you have just heard expressed in a most complete, masterful lesson by Gabriel Marcel. But Buber's erudite disciples, historians–and among them some rather well-known ones–question whether that wisdom corresponds to the message of the historical Hasidism. A few words (today I take the liberty of not remaining strictly a philosopher) need to be said about that. I have already said that Buber called the attention of the West to Hasidism, and that in doing so he has done much, particularly in Christian opinion, to abolish the prejudice that the development of Judaism stopped at the time of the writing of the Gospels. Since then, the Dead Sea Scrolls seem to constitute for public opinion (I am not sure why) another proof of the fact that Judaism was alive at the moment when the Gospels resuscitated it. As a layman, I do not wish to enter into that debate. I fail to understand how the life of Judaism, for many people, is evinced by nothing more than traces left on the shores of a Dead Sea. Buber's merits are beyond question. It was he who drew the world's attention to living Judaism. But those who question the authenticity of Buber's interpretation point out that it draws its inspiration from Hasidic legends (there is an entire folk literature devoted to the life and deeds of the Hasidic rabbis) rather than from the doctrinal texts that preceded them.

Gershom Sholem, the great historian of kabbala at the University of Jerusalem, compares the picture of Hasidism obtained by Buber's method to what Catholicism would look like based on hagiography, with no reference to theology. Another reproach leveled at Buber is that he selected the texts he used in accordance with his own thought, especially in the form it takes with the publication of *I and Thou*, and that he proved his thesis (and this is an additional objection) through the use of poetic, stirring but sometimes distorting language, in which conceptual clarity is clouded by rhetorical effects. So much for the method.

As for the substance, Buber's great mistake, according to this critical view, was that after having affirmed in his early writings the link between Hasidism and kabbala he claimed in his later works (precisely the ones that established Hasidism's reputation in the world) that Hasidism, rejecting all the gnostic and theosophical elements of the kabbala, became, in the believer's naive joy, the elevation of the given, sensible *hic et nunc* to the level of the divine. According to Buber, Hasidism "ignited in its adherents the power to rejoice in the world as it is, and in life as it is, with a constant, uninterrupted joy, inspired *hic et nunc*."

According to Sholem, Hasidism did become all that in its popular forms, but the authentic teaching of the movement did not separate the new doctrine from the theological and formal content of traditional Judaism. The indetermination, the freedom of the believer–as if the religious life were a *commedia dell'arte*–that indetermination and freedom that Buber reads into Hasidic life is, in Sholem's opinion, the reflection of the "existentialist" philosophy of Buber himself, in which, in its own way, existence determines essence. For Buber, in point of fact, life is not predetermined. "Indeterminate as life" is a natural expression for him. What counts is the purely formal description of the accentuation of the instant, of exaltation. Professor Sholem points out that it is quite otherwise with authentic Hasidism: man is capable of extracting the sparks of the divine, scattered throughout all the forces of being, but the liberation of that divine element is *the destruction of that reality* given as such and in which the sparks are hidden. That extraction of the sparks is not at all the gift of enjoying immediacy, but the effect of an abstraction. The relationship with the Eternal through the temporal is an event more Platonic than existential.

I owed it to the truth to mention Sholem's critique, which, from the point of view of the history of ideas, is certainly important; it is perhaps less valid with respect to the poetic expression of those ideas, of which Buber is fond, and which has the virtue of not extinguishing all the potential that is sacrificed in Sholem's extraction of doctrinal propositions. Is not Buber's bewitching style more than a desire for imprecision and ambiguity?

I also think, though I am not very competent in the matter,

that hagiography without theology *would*, after all, reveal something of Catholicism. Is it so certain (it is practically inconceivable) that Buber himself did not see that the exaltation of the instant through fervor carries with it a negative intention with respect to that instant in its particularity? Can we attribute to Buber a conception according to which the exaltation of immediacy would be no more than a vulgar indulgence in the sensible world, in which the lips moistened by the velvety wine, the palate and nostrils affected by its bouquet, would bear to the soul no other exaltation than that of drunkenness?

For my part, I would like to take Buber's vision of the world for what it is, even if the adjective Hasidic seems inaccurate. It often happens that attention is drawn to an important inner event under a false name, and that that event comes to belong thereafter to the interpretation of life, which is to say, to culture. Are not the instants transfigured by fervor, according to Buber (and all instants open themselves, according to him, to that natural magic to the point where one is no more privileged than another), the continually renewed springtimes of Bergson's duration? To live religiously never coincided, for Buber, with life according to a religion, nor did it ever mean mystic enthusiasm.

Filled with enthusiasm, possessed by a God, the personal soul goes astray. The contact of the divine with the exalted instants is, for Buber, meeting, dialogue, opening to others but at the same time presence to self. The instant is not transcended in the impersonal, but in the interpersonal. Persons who speak to one another confirm one another, unique and irreplaceable. In this there is a faithfulness on Buber's part to a tradition characteristic of Jewish mysticism itself. The mystic never speaks to himself in the second person as if he had entered into God, as if the moth that circled the fire were burned by the fire. Never coincidence, always proximity. Resistance of Judaism to any apotheosis of man, as to any incarnation of God.

On the other hand, what I find philosophically imprecise in all these texts (and I think it will be the case till the end of Buber's work, although toward the end he speaks much less of

God) is the term God itself, borrowed from the Scriptures and religious language, where it is far clearer than in philosophical elaborations. And that leads me to speak of the second element of Buber's work: his exegesis.

Buber reads the Scriptures in a new way. And already his reading is marked by the idea of the Meeting, which guides his interpretation of Hasidism and is finally formulated in his philosophical work. *Buber's exegesis remains within the tradition of religious liberalism and does not turn its back on biblical criticism.* But what is new is that biblical criticism does not diminish the spiritual authority of the texts in his eyes, however disparate the texts may be. Moreover, the interiorization or spiritualization of these texts is not a pretext for him to resort to generous generalities. Perhaps it was for both these reasons that Buber was fond of saying his exegesis was already post-critical.

With an expectant ear, it is a question of hearing–from the archaic articulation of the Hebrew text, and by returning to the etymologies and unexpected resonances of that etymology–the original speaking of the text. In this there is something of the Heideggerian manner. In France, Edmond Fleg undertook a similar project in his literal and poetic translation of Genesis and Exodus, but being the pure poet he was, merely by translating faithfully (that is, with consummate art) the figures and imagery of the Hebrew text. The great interest of the translation of the Bible that Buber began with Franz Rosenzweig, continued alone after the latter's death in 1929, and finished a few years ago in Jerusalem, derives from the quest for the Hebrew mystery of this text that has been translated into all languages. Buber suggests a method for a quest. I believe his method and results fall short of exhausting the meaning of the Scriptures, despite so many felicitous discoveries scattered through the translation. But these discoveries, and the new style they give to the biblical text, suffice to communicate a fresh sensation to readers accustomed to standard translations of the Bible, the common characteristic of which, peculiar to the genius of our Western languages (and this is something all who read the Bible in translation must be aware of), is to arrest the mysterious undercurrent of countless virtualities of those ancient vocables, and to immobilize the sense of their sequence in the sentences too quickly. The vocables themselves are treated by Buber as palimpsests. The point is to discover–beneath the layer of conventional terms that the Hebrew words designating, for example, Torah, prophet, angel, sacrifice, the tetragram itself, have become–a fresher meaning. Buber never says *the Torah*, but *the teaching*; nor does he ever say *law*, but *teaching*. Buber says–and it is perhaps only relatively adroit–for *prophet, announcer*; for *angel, messenger*; for *sacrifice*, he admirably reminds us of the idea of proximity that the Hebrew term *korban* contains, in translating it by *approach*. The tetragram itself, despite its function of name, is translated in a way that is rather successful, and not jarring in German, by *He is there*. Each time the tetragram comes up, Buber goes to great lengths to construct the sentence in such a way that in the place of the tetragram there is just *He is there*. Syntax, in Hebrew, does not possess the univocal interconnections it has in Latin, French and even German. It is, in a sense, much looser. Thus a whole dimension of the Hebrew text is lost in translation, and that is the dimension Buber means to restore.

I mentioned Heidegger just now. The analogy goes farther than one might think. Not just because Heidegger treats the fragments of the pre-Socratics as biblical verses. Let us recall what Heidegger said about the syntax of the pre-Socratics: the juxtaposition of words without linkage–far from representing an inferior stage of expression not yet having reached our clarity and the definition of our language–expresses, in that simple closeness, that non-articulation, a density already lost in our languages. That is even more true of the prophets, the books of Wisdom, and the entire Hebrew Bible, even in its historical parts. One really must learn Hebrew, if only to understand that in the Bible words are not tightly bound to one another.

Thank goodness our concern is with a perspective entirely different from Heidegger's! But a Judaism (and this will clarify a great deal to us in the present circumstances) that has forgotten, in Western Europe, the reading of the Bible on the basis of rabbinic texts, that has forgotten Hebrew, that is consequently no longer troubled by the mysteries of the text, finds itself confronted with a translated Bible as with a landscape without horizon, as with an excerpt, or as with certain characters in *Alice in Wonderland* who no longer have any depth and are like playing cards. Everything for them is two-dimensional. A God by projection! Hence it is understandable that Christian responses bestow some reality upon this bloodless text. In the return to an awareness of the Jewish concreteness of the Scriptures, Buber's exegesis played a considerable part. But if I see it as an invitation to research rather than an end, it is because on one essential point Buber's endeavor lags behind the Jewish exegesis as it is conducted among certain young groups who are also weary of the critical method. Buber reverts to the Hebrew text without availing himself of the rabbinic literature that is precisely what constitutes the way that text had been read throughout creative Jewish history. The talmudic or rabbinic method of reading (when I say "rabbinic" I shall always be referring to the Rabbis of the Talmud) that one may define–I think perhaps this will be new to some of my listeners–as a permanent internalizing of the letter of the text without abstraction: an attempt that consists in simultaneously inter-nalizing and preserving in its integrity the content of the Scriptures, deriving teachings from their very contradictions.

Even ritual law will reveal its inner meaning. It is a method that ultimately becomes a more dramatic view of Judaism than the West assumes, but one that, tested by centuries of spiritual life, is less dependent upon particular religious experiences than is Buber's method. It is undeniable that Buber reads the Bible as if he possessed the entire Holy Spirit all by himself. The particular experience of each individual is doubtless required by the history of the faith, but tradition must not fade away before it. It is the union of personal experience with tradition that allows the Hebrew Bible to retain its full meaning.

The interpretation of the Bible by Buber, appealing by

preference to etymology and the most archaic elements, and to the relatively recent Hasidic experience, omits the talmudic contribution. In this respect Buber seems to me to be rather faithful to Spinoza's *Theologico-Political Treatise*, which gave no credence to rabbinic exegesis. And certainly we must not underestimate the fruitful contribution of the *Theologico-Political Treatise*, which separates the Bible from any allegiance to philosophy and insists on the moral nature of its teaching, and finds a place for the word of God alongside philosophy, as Sylvain Zac's recent book has shown.[2] It seems Spinoza has played to some extent a positive role in the history of religious faith; for it is from out of these moral elements, whose richness Spinoza, disdainful and ignorant of the rabbinic tradition, did not accurately assess, that a philosophy will eventually spring, once the perishable destiny of Spinozist dogmatism is revealed. The discovery of that wellspring is also Buber's great contribution.

· I now come to my last part, which Mr. Gabriel Marcel's talk spares me the necessity of emphasizing. The justice and charity whose message the Bible bears were difficult, until Buber's time, to integrate with philosophical reason, constructed for a cosmology situating God in relation to the world and positing God, in a way, as a superlative of being.

Traditional philosophical thought covered the area of being. Being's presence for thought was the presence of some thing, offered as a theme upon which the gaze and commentary were directed. All presence which did not enter into the theme could be only an imperfect presence, still marginal, but capable of one day coming to the center.

Buber affirmed (and this is the fundamental feature of his philosophy of the Other) that the presence of an interlocutor to me cannot be reduced to the presence of an object that my gaze determines and upon which it makes predicative judgments. Not that the interlocutor cannot be envisaged thematically and become the support of a judgment, but then he or she is precisely no longer the one I approach in dialogue, but the one I consider as a number within an aggregate whole, useful for some technically realizable plan.

It is well known that that relation of presence, irreducible to the subject–object relation, was called "Meeting" or I–Thou relation, by Buber. It is equally well known that it is through that interpersonal relation that the entirety of being takes on meaning for him. The problems of knowledge and truth must thus be put in relation to the event of meeting and dialogue. The dialogue has always been philosophy's element. No one has given this word more force than Buber, even though its wide circulation since then has weakened it a great deal. *I and Thou* was published just after the First World War, and translated into French with a preface by Gaston Bachelard. It was followed by a series of works of a rigorously academic style, which were assembled partially by the author under the suggestive title of *La vie en dialogue* [Life in Dialogue]. *I and Thou* has had considerable influence over the last forty years. It brings to philosophy a new note, in harmony with the one produced in France by Gabriel Marcel's *Metaphysical Journal.* The two philosophers were unaware of each other's existence, though they were both haunted by closely related thoughts. Dialogue, since Plato, has been an element of philosophy. It is through speaking that the violence of each is raised to the universal, where, as violence, it is overcome. And philosophy seeks, after all, to avoid violence. But dialogue thus understood, as passage toward the universal, sketches out the Hegelian path that compels us to recognize its accomplishment and final realization as the instituting of a universal law and a homogeneous state. And I think what Mr. Gabriel Marcel said to you just now about Buber's fear of the state, which carries within it the seeds of the totalitarian state, is completely justified. For the essential, after all, for him and perhaps for us, is not the Us; it is the I–Thou.

The homogeneous state comes very close, by the totality it encompasses, to totalitarian statism. Isn't the universality into which all violence is supposed to be absorbed, in a homogeneous state, through inevitable recourse to an administration which alone can certify the identity of persons, the source of a new form of oppression? One may speak of oppression even in a perfectly just state, precisely because the relation of the I to the universality that recognizes but defines it passes inevitably through an administration.

The dialogue such as Buber conceives of it is prior to the universality of the political dialogue. It is a dialogue that causes one to "enter into dialogue," so to speak. That is what Plato was always seeking. If you speak with me I can convince you, but how to oblige you to enter into dialogue? Buber seeks the dialogue that brings one into dialogue. The "I" appealing to the "Thou," instead of considering him or her as an object or an enemy, is the primal fact. And it is not the legal obliteration of the *I* under the universal and anonymous law of the state, it is the use of the *Thou* in direct address which no concept could capture that institutes the just society and world, the Messianic world, putting an end to violence and enlightening all intelligence.

There is, then, a prior fraternity of humanity. And the reinstatement of that lost fraternity, a reinstatement by the miracle of Israel and the Revelation (rather than in a dialectically deduced history), the accomplishment of the Meeting in the Revelation (which is the prototype of all meeting), situate that entire philosophy, incontestably, within the domain of Judaism and constitute, according to Buber, the philosophical contribution of the Bible, repeated and rediscovered in Hasidism.

The relation between persons and the priority of justice that this implies, justice elevated to the status not only of the moral, but also of the religious experience; morality receiving as an indirect consequence of the heteronomy of the meeting its supreme dignity; intelligence springing from the heteronomy which is the very relation between I and Other; philosophy as the very life of intelligence, the basis of which is not the adequate idea: all these traits bring Buber's thought close to a certain aspect of Judaism. And I will never go beyond this statement, because I do not know how to summarize Judaism. Because I cannot–one cannot–summarize Judaism.

It is certainly the irreducibility of the "I–Thou" relation of the Meeting, the irreducibility of the Meeting to any relation with the *determinable* and the objective, that remains Buber's principle contribution to Western thought. It dominates, of course, his view of Hasidism and the Bible, and his attitude with respect to the questions that present themselves to him. Buber has given ample treatment to political questions, relations with Christianity, economic and educational issues. All these problems always come down to the situation of the Meeting. Gabriel Marcel has said that that idea constitutes a veritable Copernican revolution of thought. Buber claims to have found the idea in Feuerbach. You just heard the Feuerbach quotation:[3] I think it is Buber and Gabriel Marcel who have given it the significance that inspires reflection. Often the Meeting seems for Buber to be the last word in philosophical analysis. He privileges the special case of the relation and the meeting that takes place between beings who do not know each other. The Meeting is consequently, to Buber, pure act, transcendence without content that cannot be told, a pure spark like the instant of Bergsonian intuition, like the "almost-nothing" of the Bergsonian thinker Jankélévitch, in which the relation of consciousness to a content diminishes in the extreme, to attain that limit in which consciousness no longer has content, but remains like the point of a needle penetrating being. Meetings are, for Buber, dazzling instants without continuity or content. All this is consistent with Buber's religious liberalism, with his religious feeling, which very early on opposed religion–placing, by reaction to dogmatism, the contact above its content, the pure and unqualifiable presence of God above all dogma and all rule.

We remain, with Buber, too often on the level of the purely formal meeting, even though he adds the word "responsibility." Despite its repetitions, the word seems to lack vigor, and nothing succeeds in making it more specific. The themes of free, open and undetermined life keep recurring. The same is true of the notion of God, the moment one chooses to forget the Bible, in philosophy. The notion of God intervenes in a somewhat uncertain manner as the prototype of all expectation, without the dimension of the divine having been specified.

Mr. Gabriel Marcel has quoted the most favorable, the most profound texts of Buber on the relation between God and man. But I still have the impression that it is a transposition of the relation with one's neighbor. Indeed, it is very important (one cannot thank Buber enough for it) that the notion of the *sacred* does not appear to Buber as determining the notion of the divine. It is from dialogue that one moves toward the sacred and not the opposite, whereas for Heidegger the notion of the sacred alone is supposed to allow us to speak of God. Buber is definitely monotheistic and his word [*parole*] does not depend on the existence of any world, landscape, or any language speaking before someone speaks it.

But the specifics of the thought and discourse that thus move toward God are never formulated.

I think Buber's work merits a continuation in its most valid and novel part, and that one should not limit oneself to that slightly romantic formalism of an overly vague spiritualism. I think the formalism of the Meeting is foreign to the Jewish genius. Buber rises in violent opposition to the Heideggerian notion of *Fürsorge* which, to the German philosopher, would be access to Others. It is certainly not from Heidegger that one should take lessons on the love of man or social justice. But *Fürsorge* as response to an essential destitution accedes to the alterity of the Other. It takes into account that dimension of height and misery through which the very epiphany of others takes place. Misery and poverty are not properties of the Other, but the modes of his or her appearing to me, way of concerning me, and mode of proximity. One may wonder whether clothing the naked and feeding the hungry do not bring us closer to the neighbor than the rarefied atmosphere in which Buber's Meeting sometimes takes place.[4] Saying "Thou" thus passes through my body to the hands that give, beyond the speech organs–which is in a good Biranian tradition[5] and in keeping with the biblical truths. Before the face of God one must not go with empty hands. It is also consistent with the talmudic texts that proclaim that "to give food" is a very great thing, and to love God with all one's heart and with all one's life is yet surpassed when one loves Him with all one's money. Ah! Jewish materialism!

What Buber leaves us to ponder, from the point of view of general philosophy, is how to find a way in which a presence that is neither objectivity nor the unveiling of being can present itself. Buber's "Meeting" has suggested a relation that cannot be cast in the molds of consciousness to which one is tempted to reduce all presence for us; and it is not easy to impugn these molds. But if these molds, these forms of consciousness, determined all presence, nothing else would be able to enter our world. Now, the Meeting is a particular case of a presence that is not representation, that is absolutely straightforward, the most straightforward there is, straightforwardness itself and yet straightforwardness that is not thematized. That the immanent sphere can be broken, that an irreducible proximity can disturb the order–this is surely the great theme brought to us by Buber's philosophy. The notion that beyond absence and presence, which perhaps lead back to thematization and objectification and ontology, one can get out of the world or being, and that beyond being, and beings, one can approach or be approached, that is the theme of an inquiry that does not posit God as a very great being, nor as a human other greater than any neighbor–an inquiry that wishes, before speaking to God, to express proximity, to describe whence the voice comes and how the trace is left.

2 Martin Buber, Gabriel Marcel and Philosophy

I and Thou, published in 1923, revealed the existence in Germany of a whole current of thought that, whether anticipatory or reminiscent, more or less converged with Buber's ideas. Texts conceived along the same lines preceded or followed the publication of his book by a short interval. They were signed by Ferdinand Ebner, Hans and Rudolf Ehrenberg, Eugen Rosenstock-Huessy, Eberhard Griesbach and a few others. These authors, however, belonged to the same cultural sphere. The encounter between the work of Martin Buber and that of Gabriel Marcel is a more conclusive indication of a spiritual reality independent of the accidents of discourse. When Gabriel Marcel was writing his *Metaphysical Journal*, he did not know Martin Buber. He came from an intellectual tradition far removed, at that time, from the German academic atmosphere. By comparing, in their general traits, the speculative formulations of these two remarkable minds, so generously endowed in so many diverse domains, I would like to examine chiefly to what extent the thought expressed through their work, contrasting sharply with the style of the philosophy handed down to them, responds to the vocation of philosophy, how it renews it, and more specifically how the traditional privilege of ontology is affected by this new approach, in which the source and the model for the meaningful are sought in interhuman relations.

The relationship between Gabriel Marcel and Martin Buber was recently the object of a brilliant and profound study which appeared in Hebrew in a collection on "Jewish Thought vis-à-vis Universal Culture." The author, my friend Professor Mosche Schwartz of the University of Bar-Ilan in Israel, a specialist on Schelling and Rosenzweig who was to speak at the Beer-Sheva Colloquium on the subject of religious language in Buber, passed away a few weeks before the opening of this Colloquium. Rereading his essay, I thought that for all matters concerning the historical comparison between Buber and Marcel, I could borrow the essential from him. Thus a modest homage may be rendered to the memory of a friend who was a keen and sensitive thinker. Will I succeed, according to the rabbinic doctors' way of paraphrasing the Song of Songs 7: 10, in "making the sleeping lips speak"?

1

There is a remarkable commonality in the essential views of Gabriel Marcel and Martin Buber: the I–Thou relation described in its originality as distinguished from what Buber designates as I–It; the originality of sociality with respect to the subject–object structure, the latter not even being necessary to the grounding of the former; the Thou *par excellence*, invoked in God whom Buber calls the Eternal Thou and whom, according to Marcel, one would fail to apprehend were one to name Him in the third person; the invocation or addressing, in God, of an eternal Thou, which opens up a dimension that is the precondition for the meeting of a human Thou (even though the human may also allow of being treated as an object); and, thus, the founding of all truly interpersonal relations in an originative religion. That is the essential discovery that appears at first blush common to both the Jewish and the Christian philosopher. It consists in affirming that human spirituality–or religiosity–lies in the fact of the proximity of persons, neither lost in the mass nor abandoned to their solitude.[1] This bespeaks both the religious significance of interhuman relations and, conversely, the original possibility and accomplishment of the relation-to-God (that relation to the Invisible, the Non-Given) in the approach of one person to another, addressed as *Thou*. An approach that greets the other, an I–Thou relation, i.e. a relation fundamentally *other* than the perception of the other in his or her nature or essence, which would lead to truths or opinions expressed in the guise of judgments, as in the experience of any object whatsoever.

The object is not to the subject as the subject is to the object, whereas in the Meeting between the *I* and the *Thou* in which the address is articulated, the relation is reciprocity itself: the *I* says "thou" to a Thou inasmuch as this *Thou* is an I capable of replying with a "thou." There is, then, on this view, something resembling an initial equality of status between the addressor and the addressee. But status here is only a manner of speaking. At best, such a term might be appropriately applied to the subject and object, terms positing themselves or being posited for themselves. The *I* and *Thou* do not bear within them the ratio of their relation; the I–Thou relation contrasts sharply with the subject–object one precisely because, in Buber, it is somehow traced out prior to the terms, as a "between" (*Zwischen*). And Marcel, early on, in his *Metaphysical Journal*[2] discovered the necessity of an energetic analysis of this "between": "the eminent value of *autarkia*, or personal self-sufficiency" is depreciated in the affirmation that "only a relationship of being to being can be called spiritual." And in his study on Buber in the collective work of 1963,[3] Marcel seems to confirm his agreement on this point, writing: "In all these situations, the meeting does not take place in any sense in one or the other participant, nor in a neutral unity embracing both, but in the truest sense between them in a dimension accessible to them alone."

The two philosophers agree in questioning the spiritual primacy of intellectual objectivism, which is affirmed in science, taken as the model of all intelligibility, but also in Western philosophy, from which that science emerged. Buber and Marcel challenge the claim of the intellectual act of knowledge to the dignity of the spiritual act *par excellence*. It is a challenge they share, in a sense, with the philosophy of existence. Buber and Marcel join the latter in the search for an ecstatic fullness of existence as a whole and for a presence that, in the objectivity of things-to-be-known, becomes limited and distorted. This is what allows these philosophers to elevate concrete terms with an anthropological ring, which hitherto had occurred only in psychology, to the rank of categories (or existentials, as they are called since Heidegger). But for the philosophers of coexistence, the "ekstasis" around which concrete human plenitude gathers is not the thematizing intentionality of experience, but the addressing of the other, a person-to-person relation, culminating in the pronoun "thou." It is not truth that is the ultimate meaning of that relation, but *sociality*, which is irreducible to knowledge and truth.

Let us note before proceeding that, although Buber and Marcel, in their descriptions of the Meeting or the Relation, as Buber calls it, break away from an ontology of the object and of substance, both characterize the I–Thou relation in terms of *being*. "Between" is a *mode of being*: co-presence, co-esse. If we are to go by the letter of the texts, being and presence remain the ultimate support of meaning.

It would be important, however, to determine whether both philosophers turn to ontological language for the same reason–whether, in Buber, the break with ontology does not intimate a more radical rupture–whether the persistence of ontology in his work is not more anomalous than in Marcel's, who, although remarkably free from any school, or scholasticism, and so deliberately hostile to the objectivist interpretation of being, remains deeply rooted, despite all the disruption introduced by the idea of the Thou, in ontology. Thus Marcel appears to continue the high Western tradition for which the supreme characterization of the Divine amounts to identifying it with being; and for which all relation with being is, in the final analysis, reducible to an experience (that is, to knowledge), and remains a modality of that being. The philosophy that affirms the originality of the I–Thou relation, on the contrary, proposes that *sociality* is irreducible to the *experience of sociality*–that, as extreme rectitude, it does not inflect back upon itself as does the *esse* of being, which always *gives* itself, that is, is destined to the "understanding of being," lending credence, ever anew, to idealism. But this is a dis-interested élan, the sense of which signifies in an absolutely straightforward thought. Reflection can find only an ambiguous trace of it.

<h1 style="text-align:center">2</h1>

Already in his stance on the medieval dispute about universals, Buber favors nominalism. He rejects the tendency that, in his opinion, would recognize the absolute only in the universal, and consequently imply the privilege of knowledge. The latter, according to Buber, even in Spinozan monism is but an escape from lived experience. Contemplation, the visual, optic life–that is, precisely recourse to ideal notions. The knowledge of the object, impossible without idealization, is but the congealed form of an existential state. It would put an end to the personal fullness attained in the Meeting, in the Relation, in the covenant between individuals. A covenant that rests solely on the pure coexistence of the I with the absolute Thou, on the *with*–pure transcendence!

To wonder how such an alliance between the singularity of the *I* and the absolute *Thou* is possible is to suppose that which, according to Buber's message, is superseded: the concern for a unitary principle underlying the essential duality of the Relation. Buber's fundamental thesis is: In the beginning was the Relation. The concrete mode in which that relation is accomplished is language, which thus reaches the confines of divinity. Here "dialogue" is not a metaphor. In his analyses, Buber insists on the movement inherent in the word, which cannot be accommodated within the speaker, and already seizes upon or is received by the listener, whom it transforms into an answerer (even if he or she remains silent). The word is the *between par excellence.* Dialogue functions not as a *synthesis* of the Relation, but as its very unfolding.

Beyond the immediate essence of the Meeting as it is accomplished in the *between* of the word, nothing can be grasped that is not already a retreat from language, nothing that does not move away from presence, from the living Relation. Relation through language is conceived as a transcendence irreducible to immanence. And the "ontology" (for it remains ontology nonetheless) that is thus formed derives all its significance from that irreducible transcendence.

Marcel, in his studies[4] on Buber, accepts the latter's views, but says he does not go as far in his agreement on "the elucidation of the structural aspect of the fundamental human situation."[5] And yet, already in these reservations that appear directed to points of detail, a different philosophical attitude emerges. "To be sure," he writes, "Buber's fundamental intuition remains unconditionally valid in my view, but there remains the question of knowing how it can be transposed onto the level of language without degenerating in the process. That transposition raises great difficulties."[6] Marcel has a Bergsonian mistrust of language. In his view, language is inadequate to the truth of the inner life, whereas the *I–Thou* is lived as immediacy of co-presence itself and, consequently, above the level of words, above dialogue. This structure is approached by Marcel through the notions of "human incarnation" and "ontological mystery."

Incarnation, according to Marcel, is "the central given of metaphysics." It is "the situation of a being that appears to itself as attached to a body." By contrast with the *cogito*, it is "a given not transparent to itself."[7] A non-transparent given: the incarnate *I* is not, in its consciousness of self, for itself only; it exists in such a way as to have something impenetrable within itself. Not a foreign body! Its being-toward-itself is immediately a *being exposed to others* and, in this sense, it is itself obscurity. "It is the shadow that is at the center."[8] The impenetrable "something" in it is not the addition of an extended substance to a thinking substance, but a way of being of the spirit itself by which it is, before all thematization of the universe, *for* the universe, and thus united with it. It is a way of being toward oneself precisely as being toward the *other-than-oneself*–which identifies it. An ontological modality, a modality of the verb *to be* that is mediation itself. That is one of Marcel's most beautiful speculative constructions: "Of this body I can say neither that it is I, nor that it is not I, nor that it is *for* me (object)."[9] And yet the *I* and the body cannot be distinguished: "I cannot validly say, 'I and my body.'"[10] There is no Cartesian separation between me and my body, nor a synthesis, but immediately an unobjectifiable, lived participation. The body is essentially a mediator, but irreducible to any formal or dialectical mediation. It is the absolute or originary mediation of being: "In that sense, it is myself, for I can distinguish myself from it only on the condition that I convert it into an object, that is, that I cease treating it as the absolute mediator."[11] Hence: "we are tied to being."[12] And, conversely, every existent refers back to our body: "When I affirm that a thing exists, it is always the case that I consider that thing as linked to my body, as capable of being put in contact with it, however indirectly."[13] And along the same lines: "One might well ask whether the union of the soul and the body is of a different essence than the union between the soul and other existing things: in other words is there not subtending, as it were, all affirmation of existence, a certain experience of self as attached to the universe?"[14] Hence Marcel can say that "a blindfold knowledge" [*connaissance aveuglée*] "of being in general is implied in all particular knowledge."[15]

With incarnation, a universal structure of being is declared: Its coherence is not, to be sure, secured by a few ideal ties, but neither is it secured by dialogue. "All spiritual life is essentially a dialogue"[16]–but the dialogue is not the ultimate instance of communication. Being is tied together into unity through human incarnation. The one *with* the other of being is thus reduced to the incarnation of the *I*, placed on an "existential orbit," as in a magnetic field. The interhuman encounter is but a modality of that ontological coherence mediated by the incarnation in which the I is *for* the other. Here we are on the hither side of the Buberian Relation, but at the heart of co-presence: participation founding all relation. Participation is not a dialogue. It is an intersubjective nexus deeper than the language that is torn away, according to Marcel, from that originative communication. As a principle of alienation, language petrifies living communication: it is precisely in speaking that we pass most easily from "Thou" to "He" and to "It"–objectifying others.[17]

Whereas for Buber to say "Thou" is an absolute relation having no foundational principle behind it, Marcel opposes language understood as the *element* of the Meeting; he opposes the very term *Relation*, preferring "meeting" or "tension" (*Spannung*).[18] He denounces the conceptual character attaching, in his view, to terms in a "relation" and to their objectivity, suggested by that word.[19] Going to a deeper level than incarnation, he is anxious to replace *relation* with the more fundamental structure of the ontological mystery. "It seems to me," he writes, "that it is inaccurate to say: 'In the beginning was the Relation.' In the beginning there is rather a certain presentiment of unity that continuously dissolves, giving way to a Whole that will be formed by reciprocally linked notions." Marcel's intent is certainly not to set up, in opposition to Buber's Relation (nor to imagine behind it), some reality conceived on the model of objects or idealities or any sort of closed system. The concern is rather to establish a concrete life that overflows and leads man to the heart of his being, where the originative bond, or love, is bound. To the heart of his being–which is not entirely his. "We are not entirely ours." That is one of the consequences of Marcel's analysis of the ontological mystery: the subject is not entirely his or her own. The divine being that we are not, the absolute Thou whom we meet as transcendent, is also the being that sustains and loves us. Marcel reproaches Buber for designating the situation of the I–Thou meeting as *Gegenwärtigkeit*. It is certainly not the reference to presence as a modality of being, the implicit recourse to ontology, that seems reprehensible to him, but rather the idea of the *gegen*, the *against*, calling to mind the *gegen* of *Gegenständlichkeit*[20] and suggesting the possibility of a pure exteriority, whereas what is invoked as transcendent, according to Marcel, already grounds that invocation and the invoker. The mystery of being is the way our being which "goes toward God" already belongs to God, and it is the way the being of God holds the *I* of man. The *I* of man is no longer the middle, nor the beginning, nor the end point of the Whole.

This mystery is recognized, for example, in the question "What is it to be?" An initial reflection discovers that the questioner is already in that which he or she puts in question; the problem proves to be meta-problematic. Nothing is pure problem, nothing entirely put forward: in thinking about being, I participate, in this thinking, in what I am thinking about. The questioning is in the final analysis not *in* me, but in being itself; and the I thus discovers itself, in a second-degree reflection or meditation, as not belonging totally to itself, but as if plunged in the "ontological mystery" that envelops its functioning as subject.

The meeting with the absolute Thou is thus enveloped within the mystery of being: "The *heart* of my existence is that which is at the center of what I might designate as important to my life; it is the nucleus from which I draw my life; moreover it is not, most of the time, an object of clear consciousness for me. The heart, the nucleus of my existence, is also the community between thee and I, in which the mutual membership is all the more real and essential, the closer it takes place to this heart."[21]

Contrary to Buber's view, the meeting of the neighbor, of the human Thou, presupposes a "sharing of the same history" or the same destiny, and not the unconditionality of the approach. According to Marcel, we do not "meet" everyone we happen to run into.[22] The I–Thou does not occur just anywhere. For example, it is fear for our existence in a train that stops in an unusual manner in the middle of the countryside that brings us together–we travelers, we who were nevertheless *side by side* with one another–by tearing us away from our banal, egocentric perspectives. It is not, as in Buber, the mere appearance of the other that constitutes meeting.

According to Gabriel Marcel, the ontological mystery receives, in meditation, a luminosity of its own–precisely that of faith–which is not seen as an incomprehensible and unreflective act, but as the height of intelligibility. Through the discovery of the I–Thou, Marcel remains faithful to the spirituality of knowledge. The spirit directed toward God as Thou is also the event of the *ens manifestum sui* [being that is manifest to itself], the fact of being's self-revelation. Saying God as Thou does not underscore transcendence, but is a modality of the revelation and truth of the Absolute. As the common source of thought and being, the mystery of love signifies the immanence of Myself to God and of God to myself. It is, as Schwartz summarizes it, what Schelling would call transcendence made immanence. Buber eliminates the gnoseological foundation of the Meeting. The unconditioned event of the Meeting overflows thought and being. It is a pure dialogue, a pure *covenant* that no pneumatic common presence envelops. I am destined for the other not because of our *prior* proximity or our substantial union, but because the Thou is absolutely other.

3

The achievement of Marcel and Buber–henceforth the classic example of the philosophy called (overlooking the difference between Buber and Marcel) the philosophy of dialogue–is not only the discovery of an intellectual novelty alongside objectification, a "curious" relation, called relation with a Thou. For the history of ideas, that accession to God as to an Eternal Thou or absolute Other would seem, at any rate, to mark the end of a certain metaphysics of the object, in which God is deduced as the unconditioned, setting out from that object, by a movement of founding or conditioning. The "philosophy of dialogue" also shows a questioning of the exclusive *intelligibility* of the *foundation* and the questioning of objectification and even thematization as sole sources of the meaningful. But how does dialogue respond to the very vocation of philosophy?

What was that vocation? It was traditionally understood as an appeal to live in such a way as not to undergo social, cultural, political and religious decisions and imperatives passively, not to be taken in by ideologies–which is probably the negative definition of thought itself and of reason in their age-old opposition to opinion; and, in the final analysis, it is being able to say *I*, to think in saying *I*–the ability to say in all sincerity: *cogito*. What sustained this ability in our Western world was objective knowledge, fulfilled in communicable patency, attaining unshakable, substantial being, affirming itself on the firmness of the earth–knowledge attaining that same substantiality and firmness, in the presence, the identity of being in its being as such, miraculously equal to the knowledge that sought it, marvelously *made to measure* for that knowledge. Knowledge and being–correlation, the most perfect match! The rigorous development of this knowledge led to the fullest consciousness of self. To think being is to think on one's own scale, to coincide with oneself. And the way the ability to say *I* was understood in that adequate knowledge which equaled itself in equaling being, without anything being able to remain outside that adequate knowledge to weigh it down, was called freedom. But on that royal road as well, philosophers found they had been duped.

Let us not dwell on the fact that the intellectual mastery of being eventually proved to be the technological mastery of being as world, and that, though freed by scientific reason, man became the plaything of technological necessities dictating their law to reason. It was also the presence of being to reason–the reason of pure speculation–that became problematic.

The history of thought reflects a growing uncertainty about (a) the precise significance of the rational, once wrested free from opinion and ideology; (b) the presence of being itself as opposed to its false semblance in the forms embracing it, in which *appearing* remains suspect of appearances; and (c) the foundation and significance of science, which, despite its success, does not know from what place in being and under what conditions its so self-confident voice sounds forth. The history of philosophy is an ever-renewed struggle against the imprudence of the spontaneous exercise of reason, incapable of ensuring its security and protecting itself from paralogisms, and thus from the resurgence, in ever unexpected forms, of naivety at the heart of reflection. Kantian philosophy itself [*le criticisme*], which has lent reason its form and figure, was still misled by a traditional logic accepted as fixed, and needed a phenomenology, whether Hegelian–overcoming the separations of logical understanding by a form of reason in movement, or, more humbly but more radically, Husserlian–seeking full lucidity on the hither side of logic in a *living present*, in its proto-impressions and their syntheses and "passive explications." In Husserl's view that full lucidity has already been diminished by the first constituted structures of objectivity, which block the horizons of critical scrutiny.

Whence a privilege of presence, which is precisely what is called into question by one whole current of contemporary French philosophy, a current that may be characterized as a "merciless critical inquiry." A critique born of a reflection on all the conditions and all the "mediations" of supposedly immediate experience: political, social, epistemological, psychoanalytic, linguistic, poetic. It is no longer the worlds-behind-the-world that are challenged: there would seem to be a transcendental illusion in the immediately given, in the world spread out before us with nothing hidden. It is a critique one can be tempted to reproach for not applying its critique to its own possibility; but it is impossible to use that reproach to avoid taking it seriously. It is not a question of adopting it as one might a fashion emanating from a large Western metropolis. But not to see in it the testimony of a crisis that befalls us on the royal road of philosophy which identifies meaning and intelligibility with the intellectual act of knowing would be even more frivolous.

The philosophies of dialogue of Buber and Marcel, despite all that separates them, indirectly bear witness to that crisis that doubtless already began between the two world wars, but was not just a malaise of circumstance. I have asked: Does their contestation of the philosophical privilege of the *relation* to the *other* understood as a *being* thematized and assimilable to knowledge through the power of ideal generalities, and their doctrine of the *relation to the other* as ensuring the alterity of the other, and thus his or her transcendence as that of a *Thou* addressed in God, and in the other person met in the wake of that address–does that thought respond to philosophy's vocation?

Both philosophers clearly still have recourse to ontological language to describe the meeting with the Thou–and we will return to that point. But the question remains: Does the doctrine, in its novelty, ensure the ability to say *I* without founding it on the freedom of a consciousness equaling being?

4

Let us return, in order to answer the question, to the relation of transcendence, conceived by Buber as ultimate and irreducible in the I–Thou, and enveloped by no deeper unity. The comparison between Buber and Marcel allowed us to point that out. Language–dialogue–would appear to be the proper element of that transcendence. Can it measure up to that immediacy? Even if Marcel thinks he must trace the I–Thou back to a prior connection, deeper and not dialogic (to the structure of the incarnation and the ontological mystery), is not his criticism of language as the element of the Relation independent of his fundamental position? Is not language [*le langage*] also a particular language [*une langue*], words and a system of words in which no signification is immediate, in which all depends upon a conjunction of signs? To Marcel's criticism of language, nourished by memories of Bergson, we must add all that contemporary thought, and especially present-day French thought, has taught us about the persistence or infiltration of linguistic symbolism into the most immediate lived experience, and the metaphor's mystification, and verbal idealization. Can language as *Said* respect the immediacy of the I–Thou Relation?

But above all, as *Said*, language speaks of something and expresses the relation of the speaker to the object of which he or she speaks, saying how it is with it. To the extent that it is understood that one speaks in order to say something and not for the sake of speaking, dialogue itself appears as a modality of the I–It. Is not the relationship with the other, then, a frequentation alongside truth and objectivity, rather than the I–Thou? Which is, for example, the conception of intersubjectivity in Husserl's Fifth Cartesian Meditation.

But what of language as *Saying*? Is it absorbed into the *Said* without distinction? Can it not be examined in its purity? It says this or that, but at the same time it says *Thou*. The word *Thou* is a *Said*, but it is a *Said* that is not, like this or that, simply something it is possible to say: it is the *Said* of the *Saying* as such. The *Saying* says *Thou*–often without saying it–by its nature of direct discourse which it is or to which, in the final analysis, it belongs. That address in which, even without leaving the lips, the word *Thou* is said and *appeals* to the other–does it still have the structure of an experience and the wariness of an aim? In this vocative, it is not sufficient to recognize, as a grammarian, an incomparable *case* among the other *cases* of the declension. In it there resounds a call, an event that does without mediation, even that of a precursory knowledge or ontological pro-ject. It is all the irruption, without ceremony or preface, of informal address [*tutoiement*] which is also the risk of disinterest,[23] all the grace, all the gratuitousness–but also all the ethics of sociability–of covenant, of association with the unknown that is, I think, pure allegiance and responsibility. Does not the immediacy of the I–Thou of which Buber speaks reside–rather than negatively in a thought totally disengaged from any recourse to the conceptual systems of the world and history–in the very urgency of my responsibility that precedes all knowledge?

Here we are indeed taking a few steps outside Buber: not "to understand him better than he understood himself," but to try to apprehend and recognize him as a pioneer. Is it not that irreducibility of the association with the other to any prior knowledge that he is teaching us, in declaring the independence of the I–Thou, inconvertible into I–It? That the Thou *par excellence* signifies the Thou of God and the Thou in God–this also means that *saying Thou* is not an *aim*, but precisely an allegiance to the Invisible, to the Invisible thought vigorously not only as the non-sensible, but as the unknowable and unthematizable *per se*, of which one can say nothing. The saying of Thou to the Invisible only opens up a dimension of meaning in which, contrary to all the other dimensions of thought, there occurs no recognition of *being* [*essence*] depicted in the Said. Neither representation nor knowledge nor ontology; but a dimension in which the other person, addressed from the start as Thou, is placed.[24]

It is a dimension of meaning in which persons encounter one another, an ethical dimension that thus specifies or determines the religious character, the excellence or elevation of the revelation of the Eternal Thou. The relation with the other is possible only in the wake–be it unknown, unavowed, denied–of originative religion; and, conversely, describing a circle in no sense vicious, it is from the relation with the human Thou that Buber glimpses the relation with the Eternal Thou itself–the latter being, in the final analysis, the foundation of the former. And that is the case even if the Relation, taken by surprise in the relation with others, is extended to realms having nothing ethical about them; the world, spiritual entities! The I–Thou Relation, reciprocity of the dialogue, which sustains all human intercourse, is described in Buber as a pure, and in a sense formal, confrontation, a face-to-face, but it appears in his texts as immediately qualified: responsibility of one for the other, as if the face-to-face were, from the beginning and constantly thereafter, ethical concreteness. The "responses" constituting the dialogue signify–without this being a simple pun–"responsibility." And even Marcel insists on the link between these words in Buber and sees the response as a condition of responsibility.[25] Intersubjectivity thus appears in Buber's work as a reciprocal responsibility, in keeping with the ancient talmudic expression: "All in Israel are responsible for one another."[26] Buber's entire oeuvre is a renewal of ethics, which begins neither in a mystical valuation of a few values having the status of Platonic ideas, nor on the basis of a prior thematization, knowledge and theory of being, culminating in a self-knowledge of which ethics would constitute a consequence or appendix, nor in the universal law of Reason. Ethics begins before the exteriority of the *other*, before other people, and, as I like to put it, before the face of the other, which engages my responsibility by its human expression, which cannot–without being changed, immobilized–be held objectively at a distance. An ethics of heteronomy that is not a servitude, but the service of God through responsibility for the neighbor, in which I am irreplacable. We are probably on the hither side of freedom and unfreedom. The radical distinction between the I–It of knowledge and the I–Thou of dialogue, and the *total* independence of the latter from the former–a thesis Buber and Marcel share, despite their differences–signify that new ethics and that new order of the meaningful.

But this new ethics is also a new way of understanding the possibility of an I, and consequently responds to the vocation of philosophy. In this case, it is not a question of the freedom that a knowledge of the totality of being would ensure, but of the ethical responsibility that also signifies that no one can take my place when I am the one responsible: I cannot shrink before the other man, I am *I* by way of that uniqueness, I am *I* as if I had been chosen.

This is an ethical interpretation of transcendence, but one that is surely not always ensured against a relapse into a view in which the I–Thou, the ethical, is again interpreted as a certain mode–a privileged mode–of presence, that is, as a modality of being. I have stressed, in the present study, Buber's recourse to ontological terms to describe the relationship with the Thou, and his stated search for an ontology, setting out from the I–Thou, as if being (or the being of beings) were the alpha and omega of meaning. There is reason to ask oneself whether the I–Thou relation, in its transcendence, encounters being primordially, whether it does not name it in an act of reflection that is only secondary, whether that act of reflection is always legitimate, whether the Thou as God in his invisibility does not have a significance of sociality that eclipses the clarity of the givens and their being. Does not the ethical relation signify precisely the non-significance of being, even if theologians, reflecting, persist in finding its meaning in the trace of sociality, and interpret sociality as an experience? And to use once more, in articulating it, the word that expresses that non-significance, the Relation–is it not dis-inter-estment itself, the uprooting from being–straightforwardness of élan without a return toward self? Disinterestment that does not signify indifference, but allegiance to the other.

It is not a simple matter of vocabulary. The interpretation of the I–Thou relation as presence, coexistence or the superlative that the meaning of the word *being* would assume in the *co-esse*, the proposition "all real [*wirklich*] life is meeting," the inverse of which should also be true–do they attest, in the final analysis, to the impossibility of thinking outside or beyond being? Do they call us back to the necessity of thinking matters through to the end, and of finding being there again? Does reflection claim to apprehend a modality of being in disinterestment itself? In that case, the philosophy of dialogue would be but a specification of ontology and the "thought of being." If that is so, then all theology, all ethics, all theophany and all religion would turn out to be "thought of being" in the Heideggerian sense, or transcendental idealism.

Such is, in fact, the destiny of the philosophy that has been transmitted to us; the last pages of Husserl's *Krisis* show this to us in its modern metamorphosis and noble grandeur. Here is psychology, thought as science, thought through to the end, which reveals itself progressively (except for a special methodological procedure accomplishing the "phenomenological reduction") to be transcendental philosophy. All being is reduced to the noemata of constituting intentions from which the experience of that being is made, and which phenomenological reflection analyzes apodictically; and through this process all being is confirmed and clarified in its being. All beings, even other people. Others, it is true, in a privileged way: as presupposed in the "consciousness-of-world" as long as, along the path leading step by step to the ultimate epochē of transcendental consciousness, the "reduced" subject still retains its human condition, before positing itself as absolute subject. Husserl writes: "it is unthinkable, and not merely [contrary to] fact, that I could be man in a world without being *a* man."[27] And a little further: "everyone, in his commerce with others within his world-consciousness, at the same time has consciousness of others in the form of particular others."[28] He goes on to add: "within the vitally flowing intentionality in which the life of an ego-subject consists, every other ego is already intentionally implied in advance in the mode of empathy [*Einfühlung*]."[29] *In the mode of empathy,* which Husserl understands as experience: "it [each soul] has empathy experiences, experiencing consciousness of others . . .".[30] It is thus by a certain structure of experience that the egological consciousness is linked to other consciousnesses. Husserl, faithful to the history of our philosophy, converts the welcoming of others into an experience of others, that is, he grants himself the right to reduce the unmotivated nature [*gratuité*] of the relation-to-others to knowledge that will be surveyed by reflection. The relation-to-others presupposed by the *human* perception of the world is therefore not necessary to the transcendental subject as absolute, for whom that entire relation must yet be constituted. "[W]hen I practice the reducing epochē on myself and *my* world-consciousness, the other human beings, like the world itself, fall before the epochē; that is, they are merely intentional phenomena for me. Thus the radical and perfect reduction leads to the *absolutely unique ego* of the pure psychologist, who thus at first absolutely isolates himself and as such no longer has validity for himself [*Selbstgeltung*] as a human being or as really existing in the world, but is instead the pure subject of his intentionality, which through the radical reduction is universal and pure, with all its intentional implications."[31] Hence, in the final analysis, even the privileged relation the ego held with others in the consciousness-of-world and psychological discourse on that consciousness—which, as scientific discourse, is held *with* and *for* the others—harks back to a monologue going *from oneself to oneself,* as does thought, according to Plato—a silent discourse of the soul with itself. "What I say here scientifically, I say from myself to myself; but at the same time, paradoxically, I say it to all the others as being transcendentally implied in me and in one another."[32] An implication based on the *Einfühlung,* which, as experience, is convertible into knowledge.

Is not Husserl's intent in thinking things *through to the end* to find, by reflecting on our relation to the other, *Einfühlung* in the form of experience? And can we seriously question whether or not it is right to think things through to the end, whether or not one should think reflectively? The very raising of such questions elicits condemnation by the thinking portion of humanity. Unless such questions are only asking whether thoughts that do not return to the self—pure élans—are unthinkable. Unless they are questioning whether the necessity of thinking through to the end is *only* suspended as a result of the non-thought and non-meaning of blind passions, frivolous distractions or a lapse into the preoccupations of daily life. Unless they are asking whether the relation to the other person, the solicitation of our fellow human beings, the exigencies of *sociality,* all that returning toward the others, to those close to us, to all that sociality we hear around us, waiting for us when we leave the laboratory or study, close the book, put down the pen (all that going back in which, as Husserl admits, the ties to the life-world, the *Lebenswelt*, are retied, but in which the founder of phenomenology saw nothing more than a still provisional level of the epochē)–whether all that turning back is no more than an interruption of pure concession to the weakness of our non-angelic natures. Is not the philosophy of dialogue precisely–by reference to that which, outside all ontology, *otherwise*, but just as rigorously, has the value of *source of meaning*–the affirmation that it is impossible to encompass within a theory the Meeting with the others as if it were an experience whose meaning reflection could recover? And the affirmation that it is impossible to contain the meaning of the human face in any concept? Reasonable meanings that Reason does not know![33] Has not the philosophy of dialogue made us attentive to the ambiguity or the enigma of thoughts that think the world and the other person, knowledge and sociality, being and God together? Is not alternation henceforth the lot of the modern mind?

An ancient talmudic apologue relates the protest of the angels when the divine Torah was going to leave Heaven to be given to men. The Eternal comforts them: the laws contained in the Torah are made for the earth; they do not apply to angels, who are neither born nor die, neither work nor eat, neither own nor sell. The angels submit. Did they fall silent solely because their pride was flattered? Did they, on the contrary, catch a brief glimpse of the superiority of earthly beings capable of *giving* and of being-for-one-another and thus beginning the "divine comedy," above and beyond the understanding of the being to which pure spirits are consigned?

3 Apropos of Buber: Some Notes

1

The statement that others do not appear to me as objects does not just mean that I do not take the other person as a thing under my power, a "something." It also asserts that the very relation originally established between myself and others, between myself and someone, cannot properly be said to reside in an act of knowledge that, as such, is seizure and comprehension, the besiegement of objects. The object, supposedly external, is in fact already encompassed by me: hence the ambiguous status of immanence and transcendence. The relation to others is precisely the end of that ambiguity and of the old tradition of idealist philosophy, in which the advent of language is only a supplemental factor, a means by which to make known on the outside what strictly speaking takes place within ourselves, or to serve inner thought as an instrument of analysis, or as a repository in which its acquired results can accumulate. In the relation to others, that interiority is immediately broken open and language–the saying that says, if only implicitly, *thou*–is not just the (always optional) account of a meeting. It is the event of that meeting itself, the very bursting forth of thought dialogically coming out of itself, and quite otherwise than a noesis that projects itself through the same toward the object it gives itself.

Martin Buber discovers that bursting forth or that turning of intentionality into language. He therefore begins his philosopher's approach with the primal word, the fundamental word, the *Grundwort*, instead of reflecting on the *cogito*. The *Grundwort* I–Thou is ultimately the opening condition of all language, even the language that states the relation of pure knowledge expressed by the *Grundwort Ich–Es* (I–That); for the I–That, precisely because it is language, also addresses an interlocutor, and is already dialogue, or residue of a dialogue.

That valuation of the dia-logual relation and its phenomenological irreducibility, its fitness to constitute a meaningful order that is autonomous and as legitimate as the traditional and privileged *subject–object* correlation in the operation of knowledge–that will remain the unforgettable contribution of Martin Buber's philosophical labors. The multiplicity implied by social proximity is no longer, in relation to unity–or the synthesis or totality of being sought by learning or science–a degradation of the rational or a privation. It is a fully meaningful order of the ethical relation, a relation with the unassimilable, and thus, properly speaking in-com-prehensible (alien to the grasp, to possession) alterity of others. The discovery of that order in its full originality and the elaboration of its consequences, and, if one may designate them thus, its "categories," remain inseparable from the name Buber, whatever may have been the concordant voices in the midst of which his own made itself heard; voices as commanding as that of Gabriel Marcel in his *Metaphysical Journal.* But even ignorance of the fact that in walking and working the ground of dialogue one treads on land already cleared by another does not dispense the researcher from allegiance to Buber. Nothing could limit the homage due him. Any reflection on the alterity of the other in his or her irreducibility to the objectivity of objects and the being of beings must recognize the new perspective Buber opened–and find encouragement in it.

Therefore in my remarks on Buber, though I indicate a few points of divergence, it is not to question the fundamental and admirable analyses of *I and Thou*, and even less to embark upon the perilous or ridiculous enterprise of "improving" the teachings of an authentic creator. But the speculative landscape opened up by Buber is rich enough, and still new enough, to make possible certain perspectives of meaning that cannot always be seen, at the start at least, from the trails masterfully blazed by the pioneer.

My remarks, which distinguish differences between Buber's positions and those I take up in my own essays, are formulated as working notes on various themes. They do not supply the underlying insights that found them, and often take the form of questions rather than objections. It may not be impossible to find answers to them–or even to find a place for the ideas that inform them–in Buber's texts. But that would involve a study not undertaken here today.

2

One further preliminary remark is in order. It might astonish some that–faced with so many unleashed forces, so many violent and voracious acts that fill our history, our societies and our souls–I should turn to the *I–Thou* or the responsibility-of-one-person-for-the-other to find the categories of the Human. That astonishment may be shared by many noble minds. This was certainly the case with our dear departed friend, Professor Alphonse de Waelhens–whose memory is evoked in several studies in this book–when, after having devoted so many fine works to phenomenology, he spoke of the distance separating philosophical anthropology and the face of true human misery, and when, in order to look that misery in the eyes, he began frequenting (after so many libraries) psychiatric hospitals. But perhaps seeking the secret of the human in the ethical structures of proximity is not the equivalent of trying to close one's eyes to that misery. It is not by confidence in progress, based on a consoling dialectic or the empirically gathered signs portending a new Golden Age, that this research on ethics as first philosophy is justified. It is undoubtedly the implacable necessities of being that explain the inhuman history of mankind, rather than an ethics of alterity. But it is because the human has sprung up within being that those implacable necessities and those violent acts and that universal inter-estment are in question and are denounced as cruelty, horrors and crimes—and that humanity both perseveres in being, and at the same time declares its opposition to the *conatus essendi* through the saints and the righteous, and is to be understood not only on the basis of its being-in-the-world, but also from books. The humanity of the human—is this not, in the contranatural appearance of the ethical relation to the other man, the very crisis of being *qua* being?

3

To Buber, the *Thou* that the *I* solicits is already, in that appeal, heard as an *I* who says *thou* to me. The appeal to the *Thou* by the *I* would thus be, for the *I*, the institution of a reciprocity, an equality or equity from the start. Whence the understanding of the *I* as *I*, and the possibility of an adequate thematization of the *I*. The idea of the *I* or of a Myself in general is immediately derived from that relation: a total reflection on myself would be possible and thus the elevation of the Myself to the level of the concept, to Subjectivity above the lived centrality of the *I*; an elevation that, in traditional rationalism, passes for "better" or more "spiritual" than centrality, and is said to signify a "liberation" with respect to partial subjectivism with its intellectual and moral illusions.

In my own analyses, the approach to others is not originally in my speaking out to the other, but in my responsibility for him or her. That is the original ethical relation. That responsibility is elicited, brought about by the face of the other person, described as a breaking of the plastic forms of the phenomenality of appearance: straightforwardness of the exposure to death, and an order issued to me not to abandon the other (the Word of God). Methodological importance is given to the face and its originality in the perceived, according to a significance independent of that given it by the context of the world. Ineradicable centrality of the *I*-of the I not leaving its first person–which signifies the unlimited nature of that responsibility for the neighbor: I am never absolved with respect to others. Responsibility for the other person, a responsibility neither conditioned nor measured by any free acts of which it would be the consequence. Gratuitous responsibility resembling that of a hostage, and going as far as taking the other's place, without requiring reciprocity. Foundation of the ideas of fraternity and expiation for the other man. Here, then, contrary to Buber's I–Thou, there is no initial equality. (Is the use of the familiar I–Thou form justified?)[1] Ethical inequality: subordination to the other, original diacony:[2] the "first person accusative" and not "nominative." Hence the profound truth of Dostoyevsky's *Brothers Karamazov*, often quoted: "We are all guilty of everything and everyone, towards everyone, and I more so than all the others." That superlative degree of guilt does not, of course, refer to any personal history, nor to the character traits of the individual making that statement.

4

A non-transferable responsibility, as if my neighbor called me urgently and called none other than myself, as if I were the only one concerned. Proximity itself resides in the exclusivity of my role. It is ethically impossible to transfer my responsibility for my neighbor to a third party. My ethical responsibility is my uniqueness, my election and my "primogeniture." The identity and uniqueness of the *me* does not seem to be a problem in

Buber. They are not derived from the correlation of the dialogue itself, in which the *me* is concrete. Does not its "individuation" remain implicitly substantialist in Buber?

5

Relation with the other in reciprocity: in Buber, justice begins within the *I–Thou*. From my perspective, on the other hand, the passage from ethical inequality–from what I have termed the dissymmetry of intersubjective space–to "equality between persons" comes from the political order of citizens in a state. The birth of the state from the ethical order is intelligible to the extent that I have also to answer for the third party "next to" my neighbor. But who is *next to* whom? The immediacy of my relation to my neighbor is modified by the necessity of comparing persons with one another and judging them. Recourse to universal principles, locus of justice and objectivity. Citizenship does not put an end to the centrality of the I. It invests it with a new meaning: an irrevocable meaning. The state can begin functioning according to the laws of being. It is the responsibility for the other that determines the legitimacy of the state, that is, its justice.

6

Does not the thought to which dialogue organically and primordially belongs, in Buber, remain within the *element* of consciousness? It has seemed to me essential to stress the irreducibility of responsibility toward others to the intentionality of consciousness, to a thought that knows, to a thought closed to the transcendence of the *Other*, and ensuring, as knowledge, equality between idea and *ideatum*: whether it be in the strict noetic–noematic parallel, or the adequation of its truth, or the fullness of the intuition "fulfilling" the goal of the *Meinen* [to mean], satisfying it as one satisfies a need. The ethical relation to the other person, the proximity, the responsibility for others is not a simple modulation of intentionality; it is the concrete modality in which there is produced a non-indifference of one to the other or of the same to the *Other*, that is, a relation from the Same to what is *out of all proportion* with the Same, and is, in a sense, not of the "same kind." The proximity ensured by the responsibility for the other is not the makeshift link between "terms" that cannot coincide, cannot be fused into one because of their difference, but rather the new and proper excellence of sociality.

There is, here, in my manner of proceeding, something like a deduction of "concrete situations" from abstract significations whose horizons or "*mise-en-scène*" are reconstituted. A manner inspired by phenomenology, and often used since *Totality and Infinity*. For example, the "at home" as an inflection of the Me, sought after in the concreteness of the dwelling, and the interiority of the dwelling leading back to the feminine face. Emphasis, moreover, on the limit that the concreteness of the "ethical content" imposes upon the necessity of purely formal structures: "subordination" can exclude servitude when it is the Infinite that commands; the *greater* is in the *lesser* in the Cartesian idea of God; possibilities are beyond the limits of the possible in paternity, and so on. Doesn't Husserl's very important distinction (*Ideas*, chap. 1, para. 3) between the formal, which is empty, and the general, which is always still *Sachhaltig* [possessed of thing-like content], contain the possibility (despite the subordination of genus to form) of a certain distortion of form by content?

7

God, to Buber, is the Great Thou or the Eternal Thou. The relations between persons intersect in Him, end in Him. I have shown that I am less certain that what is called the Divine Person resides in the Thou of dialogue and that devotion and prayer are dialogue. I have been led to have recourse to the third person, to what I have called *illeity*, to speak of the Infinite and the divine transcendence, which is other than the alterity of others. Illeity of God who sends me to serve my neighbor, to responsibility for him. God is personal insofar as He brings about interpersonal relations between myself and my neighbors. He signifies from the face of the other person, with a significance not articulated as the relation of signifier to signified, but as order signified to me.[3] The coming to mind of God is always linked, in my analyses, to the responsibility for the other person and all religious affectivity signifies in its concreteness a relation to others; the fear of God is concretely my fear for my neighbor. It does not revert, Heidegger's schema of affectivity notwithstanding, to a fear for oneself.

8

Cannot Buber's dualism of the fundamental words I–Thou and I–That, a dualism of the social relation and objectification, be overcome? I have already alluded to the entry of the third party into the relation to my neighbor, motivating thematization, objectification and knowledge. But is not the *for the other* itself of sociality concrete in *giving*, and does it not presuppose *things*, without which, empty-handed, the responsibility for others would be but the ethereal sociality of angels?[4]

9

Does Buber's language, so faithful to the novelty of the relation with others in contrast with the knowledge going toward being, break entirely with the priority of ontology? Is not I–Thou spoken as its own way of reaching being? I have attempted to think through the relation to others and the Infinite as dis-inter-estment in both senses of the term: as gratuitousness of the relation, but also as the eclipse of the traditional problem of being in the relation with God and others. The problem of the meaning of being becomes, in this manner of thinking, the questioning of the *conatus essendi* that, in the "understanding of being," remained the essential trait of being: the being of *Dasein* meant having to be. In the responsibility for the other person, my being calls for justification: being-there, is that not already occupying another's place? The *Da* of *Dasein* is already an ethical problem.

4 Franz Rosenzweig: A Modern Jewish Thinker

1 The Great Witness

I could have presented this lecture devoted to Franz Rosenzweig as a ceremonial address. Last Thursday, December 10, 1964, was the date of the thirty-fifth anniversary of that thinker's death. His work, carrying on the loftiest academic traditions, and significant for the history of contemporary thought, would surely fully justify, on the occasion of this anniversary, the evocation of his memory in a university setting worthy of him. The Marie Gretler Foundation–which I thank wholeheartedly–would have had that additional merit.

But it is not the fortuitous conjunction of dates–of which no one thought–that brings us to this presentation on Rosenzweig. And I do not intend to give this presentation of his work the style of a scientific inventory, nor to evoke the progressive genesis of his ideas. I take them as a whole. My intent is to show within them the reflection of a world–that of West European Judaism, which is not a purely geographical notion, but one of the essential moments of modern Jewish history. It is the reflection of an emancipated Judaism of the nineteenth and early twentieth centuries that believed in an interfaith society; that knew and esteemed–perhaps above all else–the university, the

49

ritical spirit of the rationalist West; that had only distant memories of Judaism's cultural roots; and to which Christian society had shown itself to be mild, often friendly, always impressive by the ascendancy Christianity was able to impose upon culture and the state.

Rosenzweig belonged to that Judaism. Born in Kassel in 1886 of an assimilated family of Germany's high Jewish bourgeoisie, he lived, from an early age, practically outside Judaism. The best friends of his youth and student years were converted Jews, his own first cousins.

Having come to history and philosophy after three years of medical studies, he was formed by the most exacting disciplines of the German university. A scholar, he began by publishing a critical study of a manuscript wrongly attributed to Hegel, which he was able to restore to Schelling. Already a repentant Hegelian, in 1920 he published a monumental *Hegel and the State*, rich in insights and daring ideas, but still based on erudition, a product of his work prior to 1914. Rosenzweig had been molded in the certainty of the spiritual importance of the state and politics, under the influence of the Hegelian historian Meinecke, and *was quick to have a premonition of the dangers facing Europe, of which Hegel's philosophy remains a remarkable expression.* The Hegel who frightened him—was it the real Hegel or Meinecke's Hegel? Nationalism, national and nationalist states, a history made up of wars and revolutions had for Rosenzweig a Hegelian face. He felt the rising tide of peril, and sought a different order. He turned to Christianity. In 1913 he was on the verge of conversion.

After a dramatic night, he declined to take that step. At dawn he wrote to a friend who was waiting for the good news: "It is not possible; it is no longer necessary." I shall return to this statement. What counted from then on was Judaism, which his family was forgetting in that imperial Germany, so comfortable for the pre-war Jewish bourgeoisie. The Star of Redemption appeared on his horizon. A curious turnabout! Jewish spirituality had always maintained itself by the strength of tradition: the

Jewish response to problems preceded those problems. But now an inquiry into the destiny and salvation of Man in general, free of all particularism, was leading Rosenzweig back to a lost Judaism. The question was of a universal order, the answer, Jewish. Rosenzweig's biography is significant from the point of view of this movement of reversal and return. In the Judaism Rosenzweig revived within himself, and relived, and rethought–this movement emphasized the universalist traits. All the facile words of a worn-out spiritualism lost their traditional comfort in the arduous task of thought. In *The Star of Redemption*, the book of his life, conceived by 1917 on the Balkan front and published in 1921, Rosenzweig dealt with general philosophy. Judaism was not to come in until the third volume–but when it did, it was not as an archeological given or as an opinion among opinions, but as an inevitable moment in the general economy of Being and thought, as a category.

That on the verge of conversion in a Europe still innocent of world wars and Hitlerism, and in which so many liberals could believe themselves to be living the era of fulfillment–that an assimilated Jew on the verge of conversion, belonging to the privileged class, having access to all the values of that dazzling Europe, was able to turn away from the ultimate gesture of assimilation, to seek elsewhere than in Christianity, which after two thousand years of history was permeated by all the religious and human values of the Western world–that with all the exigencies of an open and sound mind Rosenzweig was able to return to Judaism to find a response to the crisis of humanity, or to seek refuge or a way out–all this reveals to Christians (but also to Western Jews) the power of Jewish spirituality, which, according to the Christians, was living on borrowed time, emptied of its substance.

What characterizes contemporary Jewish thought after Rosenzweig is that special new experience of the Return. It touches even those formed by tradition, but who rethink that tradition as if returning from some remote West, needing to learn everything. We must turn to Rosenzweig to learn what force can resist the seduction of Christianity and the wisdom of philosophy. I am certain that the essence of Judaism is neither enclosed nor exhausted in this thinker's theses, but it is he who opened the path to new research and new solutions.

But the characteristic trait of his thought is also this: the movement that leads him to Judaism also leads him to the recognition of Christianity. According to this Jew, the Christianity he refuses is as necessary to the redemption of the world in the grip of violence as is Judaism. Christianity is not necessary to the Jews, but the Jews, in Rosenzweig's estimation, know that it is necessary to the world.

Ecumenicalism before the letter? Surely not. Only Judaism and Christianity count, and thus, to Rosenzweig, Europe still holds the key to the salvation of the world, and Goethe's ideal of the human personality sums up religious history and opens onto the future. But Rosenzweig has a more subtle idea of religious truth than the fundamentalists of any faith. This does not represent, in the history of Jewish thought, a position without precedent, since Judah Halevi and Maimonides recognized Christianity's mission. But Rosenzweig's appreciation of Christianity, free of all opportunism, has particular vigor and elements of newness.

To me, Rosenzweig represents–by the breadth of his horizons, the freshness of his ideas and aspirations, the inner intensity of his life (cut short at age 43 after a terrible illness that paralyzed him for eight years)–the situation of the Western Jewish intelligentsia. He lacked certain experiences of the modern Jew and the modern world in their poignant and acute form. But, deceased in Frankfurt in 1929, he knew the anguish of a disequilibriated, catastrophic world, though he did not live to experience the Second World War and its nuclear aftermath. He knew the hideous face of pan-Germanic barbarity, though he did not live through the National-Socialist domination. He knew the installation of a new society in Soviet Russia, though unable to perceive its geographical and psychological extension. He knew and judged Zionism, although he did not see its culmination in the State of Israel. Rosenzweig's entire life foreshadows these great upheavals, and breaks with ways of thinking that bear the responsibility for so many catastrophes. He remains our great contemporary.

2 The Search for a Different Order

Rosenzweig's thought presents itself as a revolt against Hegel. Certain neo-Hegelians cast doubt upon the truth of Rosenzweig's perception of his antagonist.[1] They dispute the authenticity of right-wing Hegelianism, in which the Prussian state and Bismarck's empire nonetheless recognized their origins. *The Star of Redemption* was, for these neo-Hegelians, the work of a "thinker" and theologian rather than of a philosopher. True, they defined philosophy from the start as Hegelianism: theology and philosophy would be absolutely mutually exclusive. Now, the essence of Rosenzweig's deliberate and lucid project consisted precisely in bringing philosophy closer to the theological experience and attitude.[2] This has affinities with the idea, since become familiar to well-established philosophers, of the importance of prephilosophical experiences for philosophy.[3] This obviously presupposes the recognition of the existence of a theological experience, but that hypothesis is also lucidly adopted by Rosenzweig. The theological experience is not an incommunicable mystic experience, nor recourse to the "content" of revelation, but the objective existence of religious communities, the totality of the significations articulated by their very being–religious existence as old as history. Did Rosenzweig have the real Hegel before him, or Meinecke's distorted version of him? When he affirms that since Kierkegaard philosophy has denied impersonal Spirit the right to imprison the individual soul that had liberated it, when he sees the essential trait of the "new thinking" in the fact that "the philosopher ceases being a negligible quantity for his philosophy,"[4] is he not opposing a permanent theme of Hegelian philosophy, even though it may have been learned by way of Meinecke?

To an existence frozen into a system of which it becomes a *moment*, Rosenzweig opposes "the individual in spite of it all" and the inexhaustible newness of life's instants. But it is on the basis of these irreducible and fresh (quasi Bergsonian) instants that the possibility of a reference to eternal life arises, outside the petrified system in which conceptual philosophy imprisons such moments. Eternal life–it is a traditional term to be sure, but in truth as contradictory as a square circle, whose superficial contradiction will be destroyed by the new thinking. Eternal life will become the foundation for a new philosophy, will unfold into new "concepts," will restore to the philosopher as person the role usurped by his system, and to Revelation the dignity of a foundational act of intellection. In opposition to the man who has become a prisoner of his system, doomed to the supremacy of totality and the state, a link between the living instant of human life and a living Eternity is affirmed. Such would be precisely the religious order. It dominates the end of the philosophy of totality that seals Hegel's work.

The new "concepts," that express the protest and logos of the "subjective thinkers" opposing the system or state that engulfs them, loom up and signify in the "objective" existence of religious communities. Even if the religious communities group living human beings differently from the way nations and states do, the meanings from which they live, and which they live, are no more suspect than are the ideas history provides to the philosophy of totality. The world is inhabited by pagans, Jews and Christians. The "churches" are not defined as limiting one another reciprocally, but as each one claiming the infinity of the human. The life that surmounts the immobility of concepts and limits–life that, in this precise sense, is alive–is religion. Religion is not a stammering precursor of humanity's philosophical adventure. The ultimate meaning of the real is formulated–and its salvation enacted–above the level of wars and revolutions that fill universal history, in which Rosenzweig abstains from finding any meaning–in the eschatological time of the religious, an absolute offering an appropriate frame of reference. Judaism and

Christianity, on this view, are primarily two ways of relating the time of the individual, the passing of instants, to absolute time, to the Day of the Lord, and of hastening or anticipating the Kingdom of God. "The good Lord did not create religion, he created the world," Rosenzweig was fond of saying, and the word religion does not appear in *The Star of Redemption*. No one was more hostile than Rosenzweig to the unctuous and (in the Nietzschean sense) consoling conception of religion. His own is not something added to reality; it does not just happen to appear in the course of history; it is not *instituted* by divine or human decree, but drafts the first coordinates of Being. The trajectory of *The Star of Redemption* is at least as original as the curve of Western history in which knowledge springs up.

3 The Categories of the New Thinking

How to counter the sovereign categories of a philosophy that held sway "from the Ionian isles to Jena," with a new school of thought capable of preserving the thinker? What was the secret of the former, from Thales to Hegel? It was to turn away from experience, reducing its variety to what it all comes down to: to say with Thales, "everything is water," to seek with Hegel the totality in which states, civilizations, men and the philosopher himself offer up nothing but their true meanings. What Rosenzweig rejects is precisely that recourse to totality, which gives no meaning to the death each one dies–irreducibly–on his or her own. From reduction to irreducibility–that is the movement of the new thinking. Man is not a simple singularizing of the species "man," definable by an *ethos* and principles; he dies for himself, he is *ipseity* positing and conceiving of itself on the basis of itself. He is, beyond that absorbing *ethos*, his irreducible singularity; he is (like the Kierkegaardian man passing from the ethical to the religious stage) meta-ethical.

But as soon as man discovers that he is meta-ethical and leaves the totality, God also withdraws from the totality and returns to his meta-physical essence, and the world, which idealism had reduced to a logical construction, reveals the inexhaustible fullness of its meta-logical being. These beings, once having withdrawn from the totality in which philosophy, from Thales to Hegel, had unified them, are separate, because irreducible. And so they were to appear in the experience of pagan antiquity: there was the plastic world of art, a mythical God living within the interstices of being, and tragic man, a self-enclosed ipseity, shattered by blind fate.

But that isolation—and this is the second movement of Rosenzweig's thought—is not yet the reality of our lived experience. The intelligence cannot, without violence, break through that isolation, whereas in humanity's concrete and living experience, God, man and the world are in relation. This is because, despite the totalizing thought that can do nothing to overcome that separation, life unfolds: a moving-out-of-self of these elements themselves—time. The entering into relation is accomplished, not by the effect of the philosopher's synoptic gaze, but by the life of the elements overflowing their essence, forming time. Life, miracle of miracles, the original fact of religion! God enters into relation with the world and man—man with the world. Religion is not here a "confession," but the texture or drama of being, prior to philosophy's totalization.

But this relation accomplished by life is not a formal bond or abstract synthesis. It is in each case specific and concrete. God and the World—the conjunction is *precisely* Creation. God and Man, the bond is *precisely* Revelation. Man and the World (but man already illuminated by the revelation and the world already marked by the creation) is *precisely* Redemption. Creation, Revelation, and Redemption thus enter philosophy with the dignity of "categories" or "syntheses of the understanding," to speak a Kantian language. God and Man are immediately God in the life of Man, and Man in the life of God. The conjunction "and" designates a lived, accomplished junction and not an empty form of connection, observable by a third party looking on.

Time, therefore, is inseparable from these original syntheses. But it is not originally enacted as a "pure" and homogeneous "form of sensibility," but as determined by the event that shows it. The relation between God and the World is accomplished as always past. Creation opens and sustains the dimension of the past; the past does not merely *house* Creation. Revelation is to be understood along the same lines. As the movement of God toward man and human singularity–that is, ipseity–revelation is immediately recognized as love: love opens up that singularity. Not that there is love first and revelation next: revelation is love from the start. But at this point it is possible to say more: the love of God for human uniqueness is commandment to love. Contrary to Kant's opinion, love can be commanded, and it is even its entire essence to command reciprocity. Only love can command love. Love orders to love in the privileged *now* of its loving, so that the commandment to love is repeated and renewed indefinitely in the repetition and renewal of the very love that commands love. And thus the *present* is the time of the Revelation, just as the past was shown to be the time of Creation. Judaism, in which revelation is not separated from commandment, would not therefore signify the yoke of the Law, to be replaced by charity, according to a new message of revelation. The Law is the very badgering of love. Judaism, woven of commandments, attests the renewal of the instants of God's love for man, without which the commanded love could not have been commanded. The "*mitzvah*," the commandment that holds the Jew in suspense, is not a moral formalism, but the living *presence* of love, the very "temporalization" of the *present* as one says these days, the original experience of the present and of presence. Let us note in passing how close that interpretation of so-called Jewish "legalism" is to the Jewish experience of the rite; the failure to understand the latter is possibly the most characteristic trait of Christian thought and even of assimilated Judaism, which is unaware of the degree to which its reflexes have become Christianized, even if its reflective thought fancies itself freethinking.

The Revelation, which is love, awaits man's response. This response does not ascend the path opened up by the movement come from God: *the response to the love God bestows on man is the love of man for his neighbor.* To love one's neighbor is to go to Eternity, to redeem the World or prepare the Kingdom of God. Human love is the very work, the efficacy of Redemption. Thus Revelation begins the Redemption that is opened up by the dimension of human love, the work of a being absolutely singular–that is, mortal. It is therefore as absolutely singular or mortal that that being participates in Eternity: "The fact that each instant may be the last renders it precisely eternal." The victory over death is in the very instant of death: love is stronger than death, but it is death, possible at every instant, that also makes redeeming love possible. Redemption, a movement without return, pure future, completes the Day of the Lord. Contrary to the doctrine positing time as a distention of eternity, and thus as "prior" to time, Rosenzweig believes being to enter into relation, through Redemption, with an Eternity of fulfillment, and somehow future. Redemption lays out the *future.*

Eternity is therefore not conceived of as a logical ideality in which the individual is absorbed, but as the penetration of the world by love, as the accession of every creature to the word "we," without the creature's vanishing utterly into the community. Redemption is "the fact that the *I* learns to say *thou* to a *he.*" Having begun in the Revelation, it is completed as the work [oeuvre] of human singularity. But the religious community can, according to Rosenzweig, anticipate and accelerate the coming of the Kingdom. This rapprochement that takes place in his thinking between the idea of an eternity dominating scattered instants and the idea of a religious community oriented toward the Kingdom of God (and which certainly reminds us of St. Augustine's *City of God* as well as of Kant's Kingdom of Ends, but is based on an ancient Jewish tradition, which is not to say on a theology) will become more pronounced.[5] The texture of the Real is the Community in which people meet. In the system, in the state, people remain unrecognized, according to both Rosenzweig and Kierkegaard.

Perhaps philosophers will take an interest in this deformalization of time. The present, past and future are not separated from the events that manifest them. The analysis that brings them out resembles somewhat Heidegger's theory of temporal ecstasis. Philosophers will also be struck by the appearance, before the letter, of many themes of the philosophy of existence, provided that philosophy is not taken to amount to a mere reworking of the notion of human singularity, doomed to death and anguish–but rather the perception, in that finite condition, of the possibility (and not the failure) of truth. Let me particularly emphasize the two specifically Jewish traits of the analyses I have just summarized (though Judaism and Christianity do not appear in the "logic" of Rosenzweig's new thought until later). Love is manifested as commandment; the imperative *par excellence*, it commands what nothing in the world could command, love. Man is the mediator of redemption, the indispensable relay of the movement that began in God.

4 Judaism and Christianity

In order for Redemption to be accomplished–in order for time to rejoin Eternity–Love cannot remain at the mercy of the individual. Rosenzweig, like Kierkegaard, a defender of subjectivity, is suspicious, in his own way, of subjectivism. The "Community of the Faithful" is the notion that overcomes this subjectivism, which is expressed thus: The Community of the Faithful hastens the coming of the Kingdom. The theological language serves, in my opinion, to designate relations that are refractory to the manner of expression produced by the philosophy of totality, even though those relations are not (no more than Kant's notion of the holy will, for example) constructed outside experience. The anticipation of Eternity by a religious community is a valid point of departure for the formation of philosophical concepts, to the degree that that formation is based on the experience of that anticipation and not on a dogmatics of any kind. It is not the "state of things" intended by lived experience that is naively taken here for being; while respecting the configurations of lived experience and its expression in the social forms of collective existence, analysis isolates original structures or meanings, which, like Descartes' simple natures, serve, in their irreducibility, as the condition for all subsequent operations of thought. But, then, Judaism and Christianity, analyzed in this inner signification and these "sociological" manifestations, take on the meaning of primordial "structures."

Judaism, on this view, accomplishes the joining of time and Eternity by a pure and simple negation of time, whose order is daringly reversed: the Messiah has not yet come, but already the Community is, by the birth of its members–naturally–close by the Lord. (And doubtless all conversion to Judaism *immediately* takes on the sense of a first, and not a second, birth.) As a people transmitting from generation to generation that anticipation of the End, its life is but the perpetuation of that eternity, already lived–in the cyclical time of the liturgical year and the cyclical movement of the hour itself. An irreducible experience of temporality as being indifferent to history–does it need to justify itself in terms of some "objective" order that would possess the secret of real time? Eternity lived in time, through the rhythm of the hours, lived collectively, expressing itself in the social forms of that life and, consequently, transcending subjectivity and its mysticism and its hallucinations–these will, in Rosenzweig's view, constitute an experience as original as that of the instants of mathematical time. I believe, to Rosenzweig's credit, that his affirmation, "God cannot turn away from collective prayer," does not signify a magical interpretation of prayer, but the primordial character of the experiences of the religious community whose lived and socially expressed meanings Rosenzweig has the merit of reemploying to create new thoughts.

The Jewish anticipation of eternity is a closure upon oneself and a separation–the ardent heart of *The Star of Redemption.* The eternal people owes its being neither to land, nor language, nor to any legislation subject to change and revolution, intended for the political mastery of changing fortunes. The land of Israel is holy and the object of nostalgia, its language sacred and unspoken, its Law holy and unchanging.[6] Separated by a separation without borders and delimiting no nation, Judaism lives the union of all and contact with all. It is the peace of the world. Rosenzweig is the philosopher of Jewish universality, but of a universality of election, of a particularity existing for all. His apologetics is not based on any message that Judaism would supposedly be charged with delivering to the nations (it is Christianity that has a mission!), but rather on its being at the heart of being, on its being for all in its ardent isolation, which its emanating radiance[7] presupposes. A new notion of religion takes shape: neither belief nor dogmatics, but event, passion and fervor–perhaps reflecting the singular certainty of European Judaism: assimilated and agnostic, and yet, at a level it is incapable of articulating, still Judaism. Apostolic Christianity, evangelizing the world, could not remain that colorless faith; it had to bear articles of faith, dogma.

Whereas Judaism "begins with the end," Christianity on the contrary takes the chronology of the world seriously. It is always at the beginning. Its eternity is not closed in upon itself, but co-extensive with time. Only points of departure and arrival are above history. Christianity is the radiance emanating from the inner ardor of *The Star of Redemption.* Christianity's eternity is an eternal relay, a march, a mission. An irremissible expansion, incapable of stopping, from Incarnation to Second Coming, Christianity traverses the world, transforms pagan into Christian society, subjugating institutions and persons, founding cultures and countries. But ever struggling against the pagan in the world and within himself, the Christian is a convert: the baptismal waters covering a first birth, sinful and untamed. That is why the Christian must have recourse to the mediation of the arts–visual and musical–to seduce and subdue that restive nature. And in delineating the "sociology" of the church, Rosenzweig produces an extremely nuanced phenomenology of art, upon which I cannot elaborate here.

A curious turnabout! The wandering Jew has arrived; the Christian is still underway. And it is the end, in this way of understanding Judaism, of apocalyptic Messianism–since the Jewish Community of the Faithful is already close by the Lord, and has been spared the catastrophes of the end time.[8]

5 Truth and Verification

Religion, the foundation of Being, must, according to our author, necessarily be manifested through Judaism and Christianity, and necessarily in those two ways, which correspond to the two orders–man and world–that remain outside God. The Truth that is one in God becomes two outside God: partial in Christianity, it is related to the also partial truth of Judaism. Without Judaism, Christianity would remain incomprehensible, but not just to historians: he who is on the Way requires at every moment the testimony of one who never left, or has arrived since forever. That end point, in Judaism, is sufficient *unto itself,* even if, for God, in the absolute, the Christian Way is necessary. The essence of Judaism is not defined by any human borderlines, but from within. It is attested by the extrahistorical destiny of Israel, the permanent revelation of a supranational universality; anti-Semitism, which marks the lack of understanding of such a universality, confirms its unusual essence.[9] Judaism is alive and true to the degree that it stays close by God, while Christianity is alive and true as a mission to the extent that it marches into the world and penetrates it. The *Truth in Itself* is articulated and split in the human; it cannot be extracted from the human by abstraction. It is time and human effort, and the trial of verification for each one of us on the level on which we are, that leads to ultimate unity. And it is surely this negation of syncretism and generalizing abstraction, and this impossibility of skipping over life and its trials to get to the goal, that is the significance of Rosenzweig's Messianism. The Jew must, then, remain a Jew, even from the Christian point of view. That is why, on the brink of conversion, Rosenzweig, held by Judaism, considered apostasy impossible and useless. His homage to Christianity consisted in his remaining Jewish.

But if, therefore, the possessive is part of human truth, if truth is always *my* truth, it commits me and I cannot escape the call of my vocation. Truth is *for man*, it is personal. But that means it is an irremissible obligation to bear witness, in time, to the total truth of the end of time. The *partial* nature of truth is grasped as a commitment: the truth is *my* truth, which is to say it does not amount to a contemplation, but to a trial, or a verification of truth through a life. The truth *tout court* in which Judaism and Christianity are united is "sealed by God"; but this personalism of truth unfolds humanly as a history, the history of Judaism and Christianity. It is for man, in that the Christian goes out into the world and the Jew remains faithful to himself. Rosenzweig calls that theory of truth: Messianic "theory of knowledge."

6 The Eternal People

Jewish thought found its Pascalian or Kierkegaardian expression in Rosenzweig. Judaism in its integral form, with all its moral and ritualistic laws, left off seeming–if it ever had seemed–an abstract legalism, due to some hypothetical fossilization. It took its place in the drama of human existence, in Being. (If other planets besides the earth were to be inhabited, should one not expect to find pagans, Christians and Jews?)

Facing the non-Jewish world–Christian and atheist–became easier henceforth. The development of modern Jewish thought, and, especially, the éclat bestowed upon it in France by André Neher (whose absence all of us here regret); works such as those of Mrs. Eliane Amado Lévy-Valensi, in which the traditional apparatus of scholarly tomes conforming to academic rules is studded with references to Jewish sources; the new exegesis practiced at the Gilbert Block d'Orsay School–all this might not have been possible without the new style that *The Star of Redemption*, even through its initially small number of direct readers, succeeded in transmitting to Jewish thought and sensibility. The miraculous harvest that Jewish thought is discovering in the forgotten fields of rabbinic literature, sown for over fifteen centuries by the talmudic doctors, is not alien to the intellectual needs of the modern Jew Rosenzweig dared to be. The apologues of the Midrash are the outgrowth of problems; they speak of what preoccupies us today, but with a grain of irony, humor or even mischievousness, that is appropriate to very ancient wisdom. Jewish ritualism itself, daily practices, the famous "yoke of the Law" have also known a renewal in the souls and the mores of today; this new penchant for the *mitzvah* harks back to an old one, by way of an intellectual and affective movement that, though not always adopting Rosenzweig's theses to the letter, feels itself to be very close to his research and questioning.

As for the fundamental question, the break with Hegel (whether or not the Hegel of Meinecke)–the affirmation, above the state and political history, of the eternal people and its eternal way takes on a personalist signification, in which others, since then, have hoped to find a solution to the contradictions of the world. It is a very ancient ambition of Israel, its claim to the rank of the eternal people, existing outside of events–that is, not asking of them the meaning of its Israelite existence. Freedom with respect to the apparent logic of events, the possibility of judging them–that is eternity. It is not because Israel has miraculously survived that it assumes freedom with respect to History. It is because, from the start, it was able to refuse the jurisdiction of events, that Judaism maintained itself as a consciousness, one and the same through history. Hegel wanted the nations to be judged by anonymous history. Rosenzweig's contribution consisted in reminding us that the roles are reversed. And to want to be Jewish in our day is, prior to believing in Moses and the prophets, to claim this right to judge history, that is, to claim the position of a consciousness that posits itself unconditionally, to be a member of the eternal people. But, then again, that consciousness is perhaps not possible without Moses and the prophets.

The fact that that eternity is not a simple abstraction performed upon worldly values, not a nihilism, not the "everything is permitted" of apocalyptic catastrophes, but rather positively monotheism, attachment to what is highest and manifests itself in the institution of a collectivity–all this will allow modern Jewish thought to find the old themes of its tradition anew: the theme of undeniable responsibility, hence an election that constitutes an additional duty, hence a certain universalist particularism, hence the person who lives for all, and who, in so doing, resists the verdict of blind forces. All this is lived in the consciousness that the Jewish people already have, in the ardent heart of *The Star of Redemption*, of its eternity reuniting humanity divided, rent asunder in its history–a star sending out rays of Christianity which seeks to permeate the world with its mission.

The Midrash, in which today's Jewish thinkers seek, beyond the homily, a truth for their century and its difficult problems (in this they are followers of Rosenzweig) relates that eternity in its own way. Driven from the house of Abraham, Hagar and Ishmael were wandering through the desert. Their provision of water had run out. God opened Hagar's eyes and showed her a well, but the angels protested: "O Eternal One, will you give water to him whose children–brothers of Israel–will later be warring brothers?" "What do eventualities matter?" answered the Eternal One. "Today Ishmael is without blame." Israel's eternity is therefore its independence with respect to History and its ability to recognize men as at every moment ripe to be judged, without waiting for the end of History to offer us their supposedly ultimate meanings. And Israel, beyond the Israel of flesh and blood, encompasses all people who refuse to accept the purely authoritarian verdict of History.

But the Israel of flesh and blood has a very long experience of that terrible independence, that difficult freedom. Integrated into the historians' history and the nations to which the past connects them, faithful to the law of those nations with an excess of moral scruple that may seem strange–and that bad faith immediately qualifies as *foreign*–Israel retains the power to survive all disintegrations and all expulsions–and that is perhaps also its eternity. Its presence on the paths of the world–as Rosenzweig has shown–attests to a form of its presence close to the Father. What price, my God, has been set for the ransom or the privilege of freedom of judgment? It is for the nations to decide whether they wish to pay that price.

5 Jean Wahl: Neither Having nor Being

Jean Wahl was born in Marseilles on May 25, 1888. He died in Paris on June 19, 1974. At the age of 86, despite a cataract that had prevented him from reading for the previous two years, he was still dictating philosophical texts. All aspects of reality remained fully present to him, just as he was present to them during his entire life. Need I go over the dates, facts, names and titles that constitute his biography? Agnès and Barbara, his daughters whom I greet in this room, Mrs. Wahl who is away and Beatrice, his eldest daughter, detained in Paris, to whom I address affectionate thoughts–will they recognize, in a string of abstract terms, the life of the great spirit they knew, the man who, with a nobility foreign to any academic "mandarinate," during over half a century of teaching and research, was the life force of the academic, extra-academic and even, to a degree, anti-academic philosophy necessary to a great culture? It might be said that he *dominated* that philosophy on many counts, were it not inappropriate to use such a term in connection with a man whose demeanor was free from all imperialism, even that of the intellect–a man whose hold on his interlocutor came from attention unceasingly granted to what the other said and wrote. Yet that dedication to others, all encouragement and confidence, never, in its very attachment, relinquished its independence and eventually differing point of view.

1 How to Speak

Jean Wahl's thought is difficult to separate–especially for those who knew and loved him–from his presence, his person, the look in his eye. But I do not intend to undertake his portrait. It has been successfully drawn, with admirable faithfulness, love, and a concern to avoid the picturesque (which always borders on caricature), by Father Tilliette, in an article in *Archives de Philosophie* (October–December 1974), written just days after June 19, 1974. I propose to set forth what Jean Wahl's work–which for me strikes so many chords–says on its own, in the impassive signs of writing, henceforth the only ones that can signify. I propose, leaving aside memories accumulated during forty years of friendly relations in the course of which I received so much from his unlimited generosity, to speak about the work alone. But in fact I shall consider only one aspect of it–it is so vast and many-sided.

How can I do justice to the philosopher's poetry? Jean Wahl thought philosophy was not just in philosophy, and that what he was to call metaphysical experience (doubtless borrowing Bergson's notion of metaphysical intuition) is found in the exact sciences, the arts and poetry. "Until our time," he wrote in a small collection of essays entitled *Poésie, pensée, perception* [Poetry, Thought, Perception], "it has been poetry rather than philosophy that has brought home to us philosophy's first word, that of Thales: 'All things are filled with gods.'"[1] That phrase, as we shall see presently, is essential to the concept of metaphysical experience. Wahl expresses himself as much in his poems as in explicative prose or the poetry of philosophical aphorisms–poems often written directly in English. He owed his precocious bilingualism to his father, who was an English teacher. The fact that this philosopher wished to seek coherence beyond and on the hither side of concepts, but that the shadowy, warm depths of his mother tongue revealed to him openings onto the depths of "others" early on–that was surely his spiritual destiny, and it was to mark his work.

Unable to speak appropriately about the poems, will I be able to show the importance of the other aspects of his production? How can I summarize his contributions to the investigation of philosophy's past and present? This evening is not the time for inventories. But though my intent is not encyclopedic, I do want to present the meaning of Jean Wahl's thought, which cannot be reduced to the coherence–or incoherence–of the signifiers that bear it, nor to their psychological genesis. This meaning must be listened to without *looking down* to scrutinize the traces, check their logic or invent a psychology to account for them. On the contrary, we must speak of it as if we were *raising our gaze* toward a teaching that in itself precedes or commands the psychological particularities of the master (whether viewed empirically or as fate) to the point of preceding the contingency of his temperament. Is this approach one of supreme naivety, or supreme attentiveness? It is not true that in such an attitude we are reduced to impersonal structures. As for me, I believe that through such listening there can be heard, in a body of thought, that which gathers itself up as power of shock and awakening.

2 The History of Philosophy

At first blush, his work appears as the tireless exploration of the thought of others. Many of Wahl's books could be classified as studies on the history of classical and contemporary philosophy. There is his commentary on Plato's *Parmenides*, which clings tightly to the text with its hidden or visible enigmas, and renewal of the study of Hegel in France by the publication of his "Malheur de la conscience dans la philosophie de Hegel" [The Unhappy Consciousness in Hegel's Philosophy] in 1930. This commentary reveals concrete experiences behind the rigorous formalism of Hegel's system: the mature Hegel no longer seems to have forgotten the uncertainties of his youth, and European history seems to retain the acute tension of the situations, despite the figures of the dialectic leading them toward resolution and Peace. Already Jean Wahl's kinship with the family of Kierkegaardian spirits is manifest. And an unmistakable kinship it was, though a kinship with all that questioned kinship, and family, along with its establishment, patrimony, inheritance and security. But by 1920 Wahl's doctoral thesis on Anglo-Saxon neorealism revealed his innate predilection for the concrete, and his intense interest in contemporary philosophy. A concreteness experienced otherwise than as a peasant attachment to the soil, or as the consequence of a humanist idealism: rather the concrete as the horizon of life or poetry, from which principles and formulations borrow their meaning. From this point of view, it was already an anticipation of Husserl's phenomenology! An entire series of Wahl's books and courses at the Sorbonne were to draw their inspiration from Kierkegaard, Husserl, Heidegger and Jaspers.

All of this was the history of philosophy practiced with the erudition of a specialist and in keeping with all the approved methods of the university. Though the critical apparatus was more modest in the studies published after the liberation, these works remained till the end based on solid information taken directly from sources.

This history of philosophy did not become an archeology. Nor did it become part of some philosophy of history, and even less part of a philosophy of the history of philosophy. In this respect, neither the Hegelian nor the Heideggerian model was adopted. But Wahl's historiographical attention was drawn to the nerve centers of thought, the points about which system both assembles and splits apart. In Plato, for example, it was to the *Parmenides* and the *Philebus* that Wahl kept returning. There we can find "the very profound metaphysical experience that takes us beyond Platonism."[2] His was a reading with unforeseeable results, that increased the tension at the various nodal points of the system without precipitously changing its physiognomy, as if wary of those who are impatient to understand the masters "better than they understood themselves!" He brought questions back to life. Wahl's reflection sinks into the organic body of thoughts, to use Jeanne Hersch's felicitous phrase, like the point of a dart. The dart point both isolates the articulation it strikes, and reduces it to its simple meaning, its value as experience or sensation, to its pain or problem—tearing it loose from the whole in which it was already in the process of becoming the "having" of a philosophy, a philosopher's private game reserve, but one in which the philosopher was in danger of getting bogged down. *Vers le concret* [Toward the Concrete] is, above all, outside the protective wall of the system. This makes possible the comparisons that a point seen in its own light gives rise to, by analogy or contrast—summoning another term from the other end of the earth, of time, or of thought. That marvelous pointillism of Jean Wahl! An unconventional questioning sometimes dares express itself in naive terms that unsettle ready-made answers completely. What a strange effect it produces—a child's question coming from the lips of the wisest of philosophers! In many cases, Jean Wahl may be defined as the child's question within the Trojan walls of thought. Or the shaft of light shining through the structures of doctrines, striking particular, sometimes unknown points, awakening the experience of the other philosopher in the untamed state, in which it has retained its freshness prior to becoming hardened into a system, before being buried in the depths of an intellectual construction, before the dulling of its sharp, burning punctuality. Toward the concrete—the return to the "metaphysical experience" that overflows the static "adequation to the thing," beyond all positing of being, because it is beyond any position or condition of members of the establishment. It is probably the latter who are the inventors of ontology, of being that stays within its bounds—a humdrum, banal being! It wasn't the Kierkegaardians!

3 The Concrete and Existence

Etudes kierkegaardiennes [Kierkegaardian Studies] which appeared in 1937 [*sic*], certainly marked the culmination of that research on the concrete–concrete in which the features of existence were specified. But existence was apprehended not so much in its forlornness and finitude as in the paradoxical tension of the relation qualified as religious. Religion is characterized as "the relationship of the existent with a being who exists profoundly and has an infinite intensity of being."[3] An inequality of terms and tension in the relation that disturbs the conciliatory progression of the dialectic toward the concrete universal. "The here and now whose emptiness and nothingness the Hegelian dialectic strives to demonstrate are, for Kierkegaard, the essential. Nothing exists but this or that. The contingent, while retaining its nature, must take on the opposite nature, become eternal; the historical must be not the occasion for the eternal but the eternal itself."[4] The metaphysical experience to which, in Wahl's view, philosophy rises, also remains within this paradox and this tense unity of incommensurables. *Etudes kierkegaardiennes*, which describes the resistance of the Paradox and the Incommensurable to wisdom and measure, ends with a conclusion that denies closure. It is inquisitive, problematic.

But from then on the teachings of Wahl's books are characteristic. There is no radical change of context from *Etudes kierkegaardiennes* or one of Wahl's works devoted to the exposition of Jaspers or Heidegger, to a work that no longer presents itself as being about the history of philosophy–such as his great *Traité de métaphysique* [Treatise on Metaphysics], or his last book (1965)–*L'expérience métaphysique* [The Experience of Metaphysics], or one of the other collections in which he assembled short essays, aphorisms, reading notes, exegeses of poems by Valéry, Rilke or Blake, or his own poems before they were gathered in slim volumes; or comments on a sensation, a smell, a taste, or the impression made upon him by some verse, word, syllable, passing form or line. All this is interspersed with references (attraction or repulsion) to the philosophers of the past and present–and soon, and increasingly so, to poets and artists, as is the case in his works on the history of philosophy as such.

4 Breaking through Confines: The Metaphysical Experience

What is the *credo* of so free an oeuvre? Wahl's *credo* does not have the weight of a position, of what Husserl would call a doxic thesis. It emits a blinking light–the *credo* followed by a *dubito* that leaves room for a second or third equally possible *credo*. It is an alternance on the model of the "*aut...aut.*" But that succession of *yes's, no's, but's, or's*, those disjunctives that change neither into conjunctions nor convergencies (a phenomenon that strikes, astonishes and initially disconcerts the reader) in no way reflect a character trait or the psychology of some hypercritical empirical hesitation, nor a form of skepticism. What it displays is precisely truth as truth. Truth for Wahl is not some congruent portion of the Absolute, relativized by a finite, myopic subject, a lingering shadow or image within a consciousness, as if truth had played a role from the start, as being flowing quietly along, then later offering itself, as best it could, to a thought seeking truths. "It is very difficult to rid oneself of the idea of truth, but we cannot deal with the problems of truth without diversifying the meaning of the word truth, without distinguishing what is below truth as well as what is above truth as consisting in certain experiences to which the word truth is not appropriate."[5] What goes (or goes on) before is the tension of being that is beyond itself, an already completed breaking through the borders or limits of its definition, and thus in being itself a further-than-its-being; but also in being, there is a lag, an approximation incapable of equaling its own beyond–simultaneously a glorious inadequation and a glorious going beyond. "There is neither presence nor absence, but presence-absence, distance and non-distance."[6] Tension, and as it were the spasm of an identity unequal to itself. "The absolute felt in the least thing" according to the expression of the poet Thomas Traherne, whom Wahl likes to quote.[7] A disproportion to oneself that concretely signifies subjectivity: desire, quest, dialectic. But a dialectic without synthesis: without repose, without totality, without closure, without conclusion. The antithesis "can never be gotten rid of."[8] In the mature Hegel, Wahl still hears the young Hegel: "The dialectic is the unhappy consciousness, in the ever-reappearing distance that separates it from things and from itself, but as Hegel saw, our destiny is perhaps to make this unhappiness into our happiness at the moment we perceive the mind's movements to be the expression of the element of infinity in the multiplicity of things."[9]

Our "destiny?" There is reversal here. In reality "the metaphysical question. . .involves us as well as the world."[10] The adventure overflows the human and thereby delineates the human, in which the pulse of that life of transcendence throbs. May not the human be, *per se*, the original gesture of going-beyond, even if that gesture is first designated on the basis of the articulation brought about by that function? Transcendence uses the human: thought, consciousness. It cannot be reduced to the organs or functions it calls forth. It cannot be reduced to manifestation. Whence the mysterious formulations: "That of which we are conscious is that of which we are not conscious. It is what doesn't think that thinks. The body is a symbol of this *it is what does not think that thinks* and of this *it is that of which we are not conscious that we are conscious.*"[11] Consciousness and thought spring up, then, in an event they neither exhaust nor encompass, and that brings them about in order to realize itself in them. May that *beyond* be symbolized by the *hither side* of the body, of which (according to materialism) consciousness is an epiphenomenon? Or by the flesh in which the spasm is possible? The interchangeability of the *beyond* and the *hither side*–of the *very high* and the *very low*–is a permanent temptation to which Wahl will always yield, and which belongs to the deepest part of his thought. What matters is transcendence. In the metaphysical experience, beyond *knowledge*, the human adventure plays a divine comedy. "One can hardly write the history of metaphysics without taking the religious experiences of the majority of the great metaphysicians into account."[12] But God, God is what is said about that *hither side* or that *beyond*–that gap, that break in continuity. No matter whether it be "what D. H. Lawrence called the dark God"[13] or the one James speaks of in his *Varieties of Religious Experience*, evoked by Wahl in the opening pages of his *Expérience métaphysique*: when man "feels [*éprouve*] the presence, it is not man who feels, it is God who is testing [*éprouve*] man. Man feels himself being tested [*éprouvé*]": "a reversal of terms."[14] That is the metaphysical experience, the destiny of philosophy, in which man is "beyond himself." There is in this a disproportion in relation to oneself, a formally contradictory structure, a "logical monster." Concretely, it is the tension of being in consciousness containing (as the "cogito" contains the idea of God) what it cannot contain, consciousness that thus stretches itself into philosophy, into the experience of the philosopher "plunged into such an experience."[15] But it is that tension that is first: transcendence prior to being. It is *qua* metaphysical that experience is experience, i.e. subjectivity, i.e. beyond being. "Being in general," "being *qua* being," the being of beings that Heidegger conceives as before subjectivity–though the German philosopher is equally reduced to seeking in man the event *properly* issued from the "exploits" of being–isolated being, remains, for Wahl, a verbal abstraction. Heidegger's work is more important to Wahl for its metaphysical experience of transcendence, admired in the often cited notion of being-in-the-world, than for its "thought-of-being," which Wahl was surely aware of, after his very penetrating studies and teaching of Heidegger. Wahl's metaphysical experience is the *beyond* before the *here*; before the *here*, and farther away than any yonder [*là-bas*] that could be posited as another *here*. In different ways, Wahl will reiterate: "transcendence is at once the act of going beyond the object toward which the going beyond is directed."[16] Or better still, and in a way that does not remain bound to the metaphors of movement and the terminal points of movement, which are not equal to the extraordinary or "secret" element of transcendence and call us too quickly back to order: "If transcendence-movement is explained as transcendence as term, there is no longer any transcendence properly so called. If transcendence-term were explained by transcendence–movement, it would be the same. There is thus a tension between movement and its term, and neither the term nor the movement should be considered as given, neither one by the other, nor one without the other."[17] It is therefore not simply the intentionality of consciousness that Wahl states when he repeats: "Man is always beyond himself." It is a first modality–an arch-modality of the mind [*esprit*]–in relation to which the polarization of this original spasm of experience into being and human conscious- ness, the (so unstable) "perceptive immediation" of being in consciousness in the form of a system, is already a derivative [*dérivé*] event, a relaxing of the original tension, a drifting away [*dérive*].

"Man is always beyond himself." This is not the designation of an ecstasy in which one's identity would be lost. "An experience that disturbs or exalts profoundly," Wahl was to write in the last lines of his last book, referring to that *beyond* by height and depth. But he goes on: "an experience that, once the distance toward it has been crossed, gives itself, and gives ourselves, to ourselves." The beyond of metaphysical experience does not mean the universality one attains by being classified within a species–not the world in which beings assemble, delegate their freedoms to one another and form a collectivity. The beyond-oneself is the uniqueness of oneself, a new identity of the incomparable, the tip of metaphysical experience having already pierced the *order* of the universal identity in which individuals and things remain in their places, mirrored in impossible mirrors of knowledge. Being already burst open, like Descartes' *cogito*, containing the idea of infinity that it cannot contain. Individuals, non-interchangeable points: their com- merce is not economic. Each reflects and refuses the uniqueness of all the others, and this takes place in the exegesis and the history of philosophy. This being the case, it is understandable that for Wahl the history of philosophy was always the birthplace, and perhaps, in its burning compossibility of incompossibles, the conflagration of thought. The history of philosophy devoid of all finality, without conclusion, stretches out like a night sky studded with the stars of the philosophical experience in its pluralism–a pluralism in the form of a plurality of persons, of philosophers, who finally, within the stargazer, communicate in their very difference. Dialogue at last! The metaphysical experience "transcends our ordinary knowledge" and is characterized by the "variety" that would then be not a defect in that experience, but its excellence. Its irreducibility to the synthesis, to unity, is the mark of transcendence and the extraordinary. The pluralism of philosophy does not signify a regrettable fragmentation of a totality, but that multiplicity of modes of transcendence called persons. But every metaphysician is, by virtue of being a metaphysician, and necessarily, a historian of philosophy. "A metaphysician is one who experiences the experience of others, who expresses those other experiences within himself, and becomes conscious of them to a second degree."[18] Is it certain that that tension in the experience of experience is only of two degrees? And can the return to the language of systems be avoided in the experiencing of experiences?

5 Systems

Systems and their differentiation into articulated ideas cannot be excluded from a mode of thought such as this one, that claims to flee abstraction and that, while opposing the Hegelian totalization, must, in its own way, include what it refuses. Let us read this reflection, so typical of Jean Wahl's manner. "Plato says that men resemble children who want something and its opposite: they want rest and movement at the same time. It is unclear whether that is to act like a child. Perhaps it is rather acting like a wise man to want rest and movement at the same time."[19] Thus, while going beyond truths in transcendence–in

the "existential dialectic" that "moves from perceptive immediation to ecstatic immediation"[20]–Wahl also recovers the non-
ecstatic stage. And there the systems can be seen. There is the
return from the traumatism of experience to categories, from
some categories to other categories, and from categories to a new
ecstasy. As for the Same and the Other, and as for movement
and rest in Plato, Wahl wanted both: "How can one experience
that twofold experience? . . . The metaphysical experience is
ordinarily not one, but dual, and I would not hesitate to say
multiple. The metaphysician, metaphysics in general, if one may
speak of metaphysics in general, is not satisfied with a
thesis."[21] "The great systems alternate with one another in
time, and even at the same time."[22] In the great disjunction
that becomes alternation and that rends and exalts the
metaphysical experience, the system has its hour, and it is a long
one. It is true that the tension of the experience and its vibration
and resonance count more than the propositions in which it is
formulated. "It is not by the meaning of a verse that we are
taken and captivated, but by something else: the inner
accompaniment that it suggests in us."[23] The dramatic point
matters more than the architectural configuration it forms in
conjunction with other points. But that architecture is not
artificial, not negligible. The spirit "who feels the need to feel
something that goes beyond"[24] is not, in Wahl's view, in the
night in which, according to Hegel's expression, "all cows are
black." The propositions of metaphysicians bear witness to the
signifying nature of metaphysical tension. It is reason at its point
of paroxysm, a becoming conscious that rises to a loss of
consciousness, to the ineffable that is "ultra-truth"[25]–and by
the same token infra-truth–but not irrationality! The beyond of
truth changes meaning in function of the questions that
distinguish, and make us distinguish, between concepts.
Immediately concepts attract and repel and call out to one
another from Plato to Bradley and from Heraclitus to Hegel,
and they are tested by the very ones they exclude, or to which
they are opposed. Metaphysics is, in that way also, "essentially

questioning, interrogation," even "if the particular form given to that interrogation is ultimately rather unimportant."[26] There is no doubt that the propositions and positions immediately distinguished by Wahl are to be found in the palpitation or pulsation of a (quasi-tangible) experience–in which they were isolated. When this return to experience is missing from the history of philosophy, history misses philosophy. A return in which the light of distinctions transcends itself to accede to a new darkness, to "the dark light that transcends all the others."[27] There are vague things of which there are no clear and distinct ideas. There is "a domain of the vague."[28]

6 The New Rationality of Transcendence

In Wahl, the subject/object, consciousness/system polarization returns to its enigma, its ambiguity, its intensity or its original alternation. The endless ending of metaphysics in contemporary French philosophy began with Wahl's metaphysical experience. Georges Blin, in a remarkable study in the journal *Fontaine*, speaks as early as in 1948 (well before Heidegger's late philosophy had become known in France) of the "non-philosophy of Jean Wahl!" That unusual work in alternation, in which the saying manages to accommodate an unsaying, and the latter a further unsaying, has played an important role in the rejection of the kind of thought that is content with exclusive systems. It has been the forerunner of certain daring undertakings (which are not all unduly extreme) of current philosophy. It is fair to say that in France it has paved the way for a new kind of reader and writer in philosophy, and a new sort of book. With it, a blow was struck against the structure of the system, philosophy set up in the guise of a logical architecture, the philosopher's stronghold or domain: a hereditary domain, to be handed down to schools, disciples, epigones–an intellectual feudalism amplifying (or as some feel in our time, repressing) the meaningful and the reasonable. The latter are not immediately enclosed within acts of judgment upon objects, which, by their verdict, order or succeed in carrying out a seizure of these objects, their being deposited in a safe place–as if to be right amounted to taking, making a successful move, owning. Wahl was to seek a way of thinking cleared of proprietary clutter, a thought without muddle. "Raphael, Titian, Tintoret. I don't like that much abundance," he said with annoyance. "There is, in the idea of abundance, the idea of an absence of obstacles–of difficulties."[29] A traveler without baggage, he resumed the old nostalgia of cynicism and nakedness, a difficult condition in its unadorned nobility. As for knowledge, it was "the logic of pure quality which would not enrich our view of the world."[30] Rather the search for a "naked and blind" contact "with the Other." There is in that quest for the naked and blind, not a renunciation of light and of the investing of form, but the straightforwardness of a movement that is not diverted toward well-illuminated accessories, nor held by whatever glimmers. A point of light–is it a *being* that shines or possesses itself with an absolute having, or is it the impact of a breakthrough, the beyond of being with neither having nor being? That breakthrough has an aspect other than destructive. Not that it should be designated as *constructive*, despite the expression "autoconstructive" used by Wahl[31] to avoid a facile nihilism. The meaningful is not expressed in architectural terms, is not architectonic. Let us think it through to its ultimate consequences. Wahl's new wisdom, his new rationality–is not the wisdom of building. It does not tend toward habitation, does not stay home. Wahl was to say: "To build a house of flame. An element of the perverse, the barbarous. To consent to the annihilation of the most precious values."[32] There is a wandering and an inextinguishable pain in the privilege of the human: "The desire of the outline and the pain of color (the pain of the outline and pleasure of color) ... a burning. A wound quivers in the depths of the universe. All our pain, all our pleasure are the singeing of our wings in that flame. The reverberation of that wound within us. The spreading of that fire."[33] To ask of such a movement–with all its denial of domicile, finality and outcome–whether it is skepticism or faith, would be to fail to understand the order (or disorder) of its inadequation to being and nothingness. "Transcendence escaped us the moment we were about to seize it (unless, in the depths of ourselves, of our desire, it is transcendence that we find)," writes Wahl, commenting on Nietzsche.[34]

Thus transcendence is perhaps the essential element of Wahl's teachings–but a transcendence indifferent to hierarchy. A bursting toward the heights or a descent toward the depths of the sensible world; trans-ascendance and trans-descendence are purely, and pure, transcendencies. Wahl said this forcefully in his famous communication of December 4, 1937, to the Société Française de Philosophie.[35] Was Pascal then wrong in speaking of two infinities? At either extremity of being, is it not the same ex-cession, the same transcendence, the height beyond all climbing and descent that stand opposed to one another in the world and its values? This taste for the abysmal, this happiness of the chasm, the underground, the subhuman that is not animal, that humanness alone makes possible! "Thus there is a meaning [*sens*] of the low that develops at the same time as the meaning of the high. I have been given back to the earth, said Rimbaud; and to the subterranean, the roots."[36] In his *Traité de métaphysique* of 1953 (p. 716), Wahl speaks of a negativity beyond Hegel's negativity, "answering to the need of the existent to annihilate his thought in an attitude of submission to the dominant and *overarching* transcendence, which is, moreover, that of no dogma or philosophical system!" (My emphasis on *overarching*.)

There is in this transcendent movement an accomplishing of oneself that is at once a destruction of oneself, a failure that is triumph. We have already noted this defection of identity and this new birth of the soul to itself in a failure that is triumph. Triumph or "self-construction" outside the world fixed in being and having. Before belonging to the empire of Nature or to the self-awareness of Spirit, it is in breaking through the border of being that the logically unjustifiable uniqueness of the human

person is identified. It is probably to this that the closing
question of the *Traité de métaphysique* refers. "Will the
philosopher have the strength finally to transcend transcendence
itself and to fall valiantly into immanence without letting the
value of his effort of transcendence be lost? Man is always
beyond himself. But that being-beyond-oneself must finally be
conscious of being itself the source of that beyond, and thus
transcendence doubles back toward immanence."[37]

Should that "doubling back" be understood as the result of a
jolt against the barrier of a closed avenue, and thus as a
philosophical denunciation of transcendence and of its promo-
tion to the rank of the ultimate concept of wisdom? Would it
not be more fitting to interpret it as the abandoning of the
mythical image of transcendence born of the stubborn
faithfulness to identity taken as the unchangeable beginning of
wisdom? The metaphysical experience would retain the irreducible
(i.e. religious), initial and final heteronomy of transcendence:
subjectivity, from beginning to end, older and younger than
logical identity, would signify "the absolute felt in a very small
thing." "An intense, felt absolute. Not the absolute of the
philosophers, but that of a passion or a verse."[38] Immanence
would then signify the stage of that experience at which man
will no longer need, in his relation to the beyond, to have
recourse–thanks to the supreme possibilities of philosophy–to
any cult. A religion in which man himself will be temple and
liturgy. All external forms of worship would be but the
theatre–the acting out or production–of transcendence. Which
rules out neither the dignity nor perhaps the empirical or
intellectual necessity of the theatre.

These are two interpretations that constitute a disjunction
that must not be gone beyond, and the terms of which alternate.
But must one not remain attentive to the meaning of the divine
that shines forth at the moment when the second term of the
alternative is true? Without distinction between high and low, or
without a theology that fixes a hierarchy–here is a point of
rupture, a shaking of the depths of simple tangency felt at the

unique point that becomes myself, before concepts come to release me from this sudden emotion or this tangency. Is this the birth of a new religion or the return to forgotten sources? The singeing of our wings in a flame flickering in the depths of the universe is not the only metaphor for this ambiguous contact. Everything alternates in the metaphysical experience. At the end of the book dedicated to it,[39] a "dark light" transcends particular things. Oh, that dark light cast by the stars! It must be recognized. Not an insufficient light. A blinding light at the heart of the star, gathered there, in the form of darkness, hiding, in order not to offend our gaze or be offended by it. In the scintillation or twinkling, in the *Schimmern* of the stars, the light at its height, its breaking point, becomes the secret of flashing light that beckons us. This pulsing light–this *Other* in the *Same*–this transcendence, this awakening of the *Same* by the *Other*, this pointillism of light, made acute by this twinkling–is it not the *ineffable* in which a spoken word deafening our ears falls silent at the very heart of the words we hear? An ineffable that Wahl so often places above discourse, in his texts. An ineffable saying also known by an old psalm (Psalm 19: 2–5): "The heavens declare the glory of God, and the firmament showeth his handiwork; Day unto day uttereth speech, And night unto night revealeth knowledge; There is no speech, there are no words, Neither is their voice heard."

6 Vladimir Jankélévitch

Vladimir Jankélévitch had a certain way of speaking; a bit haltingly, in such a way that, in the perfect clarity of the statement, each word sprang up new, as if unforeseeable in the word that preceded it. As if, here, thought never left the flowing waters of its spontaneity, mistrusting the facile aspects of language, its verbal habits and its rhetoric. An original thought–from the depths–but a poetic thought as well: inspired words, which is to say a thought that, by some marvel, only keeps or recreates the secrets of its source in the act of expression. That is how I heard Jankélévitch even in his everyday utterances–how his public lectures on philosophy rang out, or his musical commentaries with piano accompaniment, or his indefatigable interventions on behalf of the "humiliated and offended," and the rights of man. The rhythm and breath of his spoken words still orchestrate, for my ears, the printed pages of his work. A work that is ample, original and varied, nourished by an immense culture (philosophical, literary and musical), initiated no doubt to the untranslatable by a knowledge of both ancient and modern languages, including Russian. Because of that interiority opening initially, as one approached him, in quasi-impassible forms of welcome, and his somewhat cool, sincere courtesy–because of the profound chant of that poetry or music, apparent beneath the rigorously coherent concatenation of his written or oral discourse, as much as for the incomparable intrinsic quality of a philosophical message royally indifferent to the fluctuating intellectual "climate" of his time, Professor Jankélévitch held a very special place in the minds of students and the entire intelligentsia of his generation. A place apart, already recognized as such at every stage of his career, from the Ecole Normale Supérieure to the Sorbonne. In whatever circles and in whatever capacity he moved, Vladimir Jankélévitch was, in addition to the allegiances, categories and functions to which his person might lay claim. . .Vladimir Jankélévitch. The proof of intellectual gifts so abundant in him, the proximity one immediately felt of a presence that was gracious, exacting of himself (which is probably the very modality of ethics), blended, in the minds of those who knew him, into an impression and memory of a certain charm of luminosity, loftiness and purity difficult to formulate.

His courses at the university attracted many people, even if the disquisition to be heard at times–or often–turned to an order of ideas not on the exam. And at the Collège Philosophique which was founded by my unforgettable friend Jean Wahl on the Montagne Sainte-Geneviève (when France was reviving just after the Liberation) to train philosophers for the adventure of a philosophy without "a curriculum," crowds of both students and non-students came and kept coming (I witnessed it) to listen to Jankélévitch, whose discourse broke with all conventionality.

Almost Nothing

The non-inscribed: the unthought, as one says these days in Paris. But worse (or better) than that: his teaching tended toward what had not yet entered into the "good consciousness" of ideas already in possession of their "objects." It risked going toward the lived aspect of life, in its original freedom, which cannot be content within the Same of the "ready-made" and the placidity of the present. A life that ceaselessly begins again, reinventing itself, where "passing" moments cannot, in their becoming, stop to be named and known. Moments of lived life, moments of duration! Compared with the well-established and measured (down to no matter how many decimal places) reality grasped by the ideas of science, these moments are almost nothing. Almost nothing or "I know not what," that cannot be locked up in the rigid framework of "clearly defined ideas." Does not the expression of the meaning of this "I know not what" call for a new way of thinking and speaking? And is this not the problem of philosophy itself, affording a glimpse of itself before the appearance of things, substances and general ideas? To seek a meaning in a domain in which there is as yet nothing consistent, capable of responding or corresponding to the poorest or most indeterminate of questions: the What? But are we not thereby already at the very level of origins?

Through the originality of his problematics and its formulation, Jankélévitch joined and prolonged one of the great moments in the history of contemporary philosophy: the work of Henri Bergson. A work whose revolutionary and glorious repercussions at the turn of the century (influencing all forms of intellectual activity and spiritual life both in France and throughout the world) the new generation seems–or wants–to forget.

Ethics

Bergson discovered–by a "return to the immediate givens of consciousness," behind the time of our sciences, which unfold necessities written in "eternal reality," in invariable being persisting in its being, and the model of all intelligibility–the primordial importance of the time of our lives, of concrete duration, which for each of us signifies the incessant possibility of enterprise, creation and self-renewal, the time of freedom and the future. He described the former [scientific time] as issuing from and degenerating within the latter. But the immediate givens of consciousness, that made the discovery possible, were already contained within the duration they revealed. Human time and duration are not only, in Bergson's view, the primordial event of intelligibility [*sensé*], replacing in that role invariable, absolute being, but also original understanding. With the advent of Bergson–in opposition to the entire tradition, issuing from the Greeks, of reason isolating and identifying the categories of being–it is the human, free time of duration that is declared to be first philosophy.

Vladimir Jankélévitch devoted one of his most beautiful books to Bergson's thought. But his entire work is an extraordinary way of remaining true to the new intelligibility and new understanding of duration, emphasizing its ethical meaning through extremely subtle analyses.

The duration of human, free time is no longer "the moving image of an immobile eternity"; but its freedom is not the equivalent of the pure negativity of an interrupted time or a lost time. It seems–sublimely counterbalancing that proud, unruffled eternity so sure of being in full possession of its being–to take the form of a worrying about the other, a spending without counting, a generosity, goodness, love, obligation toward others. A generosity without recompense, a love unconcerned with reciprocity; duty performed without the "salary" of a good-conscience-for-a-duty-performed, without even the good conscience of being the bad-conscience-of-the-duty-not-performed! All duties are incumbent upon me, all rights first due to others. That is the dis-inter-estment of duration and a summary (if possible!) of Jankélévitch's ethics. It is an ethics without eudemonism, and one that would be the very "temporalization" of time, so to speak. And yet it includes joy and a way of being open to art and the beautiful, but not as pleasure or self-satisfaction resulting from its own virtues! It is as if Jankélévitch were an astonishing magician, able to divine the words of the Talmud! Did he somehow read the words of Antigonus, a disciple of Simon the Just, in the Tractate Abot [Mishnah], who teaches: "Do not be like the servants who serve their master for a salary, but like servants who serve without any expectation of remuneration"? Did he read, in that excerpt from the Mishnah in Sanhedrin 37a: "Every man is obligated to think that the entire universe had been created because of him"; which Rabbi Chaim of Volozhin, an eighteenth-century Lithuanian rabbi, understood in the following way. "Every man is obligated to think that the subsistence of the entire universe depends exclusively on him, that he is responsible for it."

It seemed important to me to point out the tie–and precisely on the basis of that ethics rigorously conceived as first philosophy–between Vladimir Jankélévitch and Judaism. For everyone knows the role that that philosopher played in the Resistance, where he fought against the aggressor as a Frenchman and a Jew equally. No one is unaware that he condemned, beyond any possibility of pardon, the crime and the criminals of the Holocaust or Shoah. Jankélévitch never consented to the trivializing of these atrocities committed by Europeans in a Christian Europe, to view them, as sociologists, as a particular case of xenophobia or racism. The horror of the crime committed against the human person and human life was no doubt the essence of what prompted the extreme firmness of Jankélévitch's condemnation; but the Passion of Israel under Adolf Hitler certainly affected him in a religious way. Nor could the faithful affection he bore the State of Israel remain neutral from the religious point of view, despite the reservations he has allowed himself to express about the political actions of the Hebrew state that did not appear to him in keeping with prophetic inspiration; even though he was only to know that inspiration through texts translated or transposed into the language of humanist ethics–an ethics that to him was nonetheless first philosophy.

Israel Present

A religion with neither rites, nor worship, nor Hebrew. Stigmatizing hypocrisy, he continued to call it pharisaism, forgetting the origin of the word. A religion with, or without,

God? Surely only God can decide. Everything in the life and background of this great mind connected him, through French culture, to the already universal vision to which Jewish wisdom lends itself so readily, with the exception of its untranslatable enigmas. Nothing could bring our square letters back to him. The two Jewish syllables of his name were exiled Hebrew! The ethics of Judaism could be familiar to him only in the forms it had taken in Christian and lay texts: Saint Augustine, Pascal and Russian novelists and poets, Pushkin, Tolstoy, Tyutchev, and the French moralists, and all the biblical elements contained in the principles of 1789. How many other great names!

But Israel does not easily relinquish her noble, upright, pure sons. She remains religiously present to them by all the bodily presence of her history, by her patience in hope, by the presence of her dead, by her children chanting the mysterious syllables of biblical verses at school, where their meaning is renewed daily.

7 The Meaning of Meaning

Most of the papers read and discussed at the Collège des Irlandais [College of the Irish] in Paris during the June 24th, 1979 session on the general theme "Heidegger and Theology" struck me by the parallelism, or at least by the non-convergence, which quickly became apparent between the developments devoted to each of the two themes contained in the title. Was it a question of two mental realms? Of thoughts incapable of being brought together, to be entered into only consecutively? There was no attempt on either side (as if it were an impossibility) to seek a broadening of the notion of *meaning*, which, beyond the superannuated dream of an agreement between the propositions of reason and those of faith, might establish the unity in which the meaningfulness of the thought of being would converge with what assumes meaning on the basis of biblical texts, or vice versa. What, after all, does the thought of being mean, in relation to the *ultimateness* of the religious message, which the voice of theology continues to assert. On the theologians' side, they sometimes went so far as to ask no more of Heidegger than "speculative gestures," whose novelty might serve to renew religious thought, as if the mode of intelligibility suggested by the Scriptures, unlike the one going back to the pre-Socratics, were incapable, once separated from faith, of retaining any vigor or intellectual fecundity of its own; as if the dignity of thought deteriorated as soon as it was detached from certain incommunicable states of the soul. The position of the Heideggerians was perhaps simpler: they questioned the necessity of the biblical tradition for thought properly so called. One came away having to wonder whether the last chance of unity between the different forms of spirit that manifested themselves in this way could be anything more than the meeting of colloquia, whether it could go beyond the dialogue itself and the time it lasts, and be something other than the friendly proximity between people speaking, its transcription into book form, and the memories of hours spent together. Which, in a certain sense (but only in a certain sense) would also favor the biblical order of meaning.

However radical the destruction of metaphysics may be in Heidegger's thought of being, it is still Western metaphysics that remains the soil his thought turns over or works. It is being, *esse*, in its ess*a*nce, in its perseverance, in its event (even though it may hide or remain unrecognized in beings) that–throughout that entire history of philosophy, the history of a kind of knowledge–constituted the ultimate referent of meaning and thought. Hence Heidegger's requirement, presented as an imperative by his followers, of deriving the meaning of the word God from the understanding of being in which the sacred and the divine announce themselves, agrees with the main tendency of traditional philosophy, which is theoretical. The Good beyond being, despite the vigor of so many of Plato's daring expressions, will continue to be interpreted on the basis of the truth of being, and, in Heidegger, on the basis of the ontological difference; indifference to the being[1] of that *beyond*, that transcendence, would amount to pure non-meaning.

Yet I would ask whether that transcendence does not retain, more rightfully, an irreducibly ethical meaning that dominates the verses of the Bible–without thereby displaying childlike naivety or the superstructure of layers of meaning covering rigorously ontological thoughts, which alone would be original, alone worthy of being called thoughts. Does not transcendence take on a meaning ultimately older than, and in any case different from, the one attributed to it by the *ontological difference*? It signifies in my responsibility for the other man, from the start my neighbor or my brother. An ethical meaning of the relation to the other, answering, in the form of responsibility before the face, to the *invisible that requires me*; answering to a demand that puts me in question and comes to me from *I know not where*, nor when, nor why. A responsibility for the other "my likeness, my brother,"[2] who is, however, sufficiently *different* from me for me to continue to hear from within me the Cain-like refusal to be his keeper. Fraternity in the human, but already the condition–or incondition–of hostage obliged to answer for the *freedom* of the other, for that which, after all, "does not concern me." A responsibility that no experience, no appearance, no knowledge comes to found; a responsibility without guilt, but in which, before the face, I find myself exposed to an accusation that the alibi of my alterity cannot annul. The truth that accuses, "*veritas redarguens*" of book ten of Saint Augustine's *Confessions*, which was quoted at the Collège des Irlandais in a Heideggerian perspective, would be consonant with the one I have in mind here.

A calling into question that cannot be interpreted as an event, whether essential or accidental, marking the intrigue of the being of beings. A calling into question in which the question springs forth older than the one about the meaning of the being of beings; a calling into question in which the very problematic nature of the question, perhaps, emerges. Not the questionable nature of the question that asks: "Why is there being rather than nothingness?" but of the question that is contranatural, against the very naturalness of nature: "Is it just to be?" Bad conscience! The most repressed question, but older than that which seeks the meaning of being. The latter, in the finitude and anguish of nothingness, remains within the good conscience of the *conatus*, of perseverance in being, which asks no question. The legitimacy of being, a question hidden within the most banal and most troubling question, the one that seeks the "meaning of life," without being content with biological, psychological and sociological finalities of existence. A question by which the meaning of the meaningful originally means; a meaning that cannot be defined simply by the formalism of the logical structure of the reference, moving from any given signifier to its signified; or, more precisely, a meaning in which the reference is at its source in all the concreteness of the one-for-the-other of human fraternity. Meaning of the meaningful, which shows no lack in relation to an ideal of adequation borrowed from the domain of knowledge nor from the fullness of an intuitively revealed presence. The one-for-the-other of fraternity, which does not mean a privation of coincidence or of some sort of fusion, nor a finality failing to reach its goal. It is a semantics of proximity, of sociality that does not lead back to ontology, that is not based on the experience of being and in which meaning is not defined formally, but by an ethical relation to the other person in the guise of responsibility for him or her.

It is on the basis of that concreteness that the question of being's legitimacy presupposing a law must be grasped. For the law itself expresses my responsibility for the other to which I am bound in response to that demand that puts me in question, in the question contained in that demand (which the question always implies) and which, by the face of the other, comes to me from I know not where.

Might one counter that a knowledge of the other, a thought directed toward a being and presupposing the understanding of the being of that being upon which (but only subsequently) ethical strata would be superimposed, is the precondition of that responsibility? According to that way of thinking, the other does show himself, but in "appresentation":[3] always announced by signs, gestures, facial expressions, language and works. Compared to the knowledge the other man can have of himself, appresentation is but a diminished knowledge. But is not the secret of the face the other side of a different way of thinking—one more ambitious, and presenting a different configuration than that of knowledge-thinking? The face is not a form offered to serene perception. Immediately it summons me, claims me, recalls me to a responsibility I incurred in no previous experience.

Is it certain that the ultimate and proper meaning of the human signifies in its exhibition, in the manifestation of the manifested for *myself* (which is the way this meaning is thought), in guise of a thought revealing the truth of being? Is it so certain that man does not have his meaning beyond what he can be and what he can show himself? Does that meaning not show itself as meaning precisely as secret of the face–open, that is, exposed, without defense? Strangeness of the other, in that it is precisely by that strangeness that he or she puts me in question by demanding of me with a demand that comes to me I know not whence, or from an unknown God who loves the stranger. Face or non-autochthony. The consciousness of that inassimilable strangeness of the other, the bad conscience of my responsibility, the bad conscience of that difference of the non-additive other, and of that non-in-difference-for-the-other-in-me (or of my "me")–that is no doubt the very meaning of the face, its original speech. In it there can be heard the *demand* that keeps me in question and elicits my response or my responsibility. Before all perseverance in being and repose in the self, it is, in the identity of the self, the for-the-other that sobers up [*dégrise*] its identity–and never stops doing so–in awakening it to the psychism of thought. A meaning, I say, beyond what man can be and show of himself: the face is meaning of the beyond. Not sign or symbol of the beyond; the latter allows itself to be neither indicated nor symbolized without falling into the immanence of knowledge. The meaning of the face is not a species whose indication or symbolism would be the genus. The face is alone in translating transcendence. Not to provide the proof of the existence of God, but the indispensable cir- cumstance of the meaning of that word, of its first statement. Of the first prayer, of the first liturgy. A Transcendence that is inseparable from the ethical *circumstances* of the responsibility for the other, in which the thought of the unequal is thought, which is no longer in the imperturbable correlation of the noesis and the noema, which is no longer the thought of the same. But, as non-transferable responsibility, it has received its uniqueness of self from the epiphany of the face in which a different requirement than that of the ontologies is taking on meaning.

One can detach from it, or isolate from it, and think the idea of God on its own. One can think it or know it while forgetting the ethical circumstances of its meaning and even find within it–but after the fact and through reflection–a religious experience. Religions and theologies live from that abstraction, as do mystics from that isolation. But so do religious wars.

8 On Intersubjectivity: Notes on Merleau-Ponty

Husserl's transcendental reduction: phenomenology's methodical return upstream, starting out from the world as it appears in itself to natural or naive consciousness, toward "absolute consciousness," the ascent to the "I think," which is assured of its noetic being and in which ("in parentheses," in the form of a noematic correlate), the things of the world are constituted—this is, according to Merleau-Ponty, an operation as necessary for isolating fields of irreducibility as for interpreting the appearance of "just things" (*bloße Sachen*) in their "constitution by the *cogito*."[1] The irreducibility of these fields, in his view, does not reside in the exhibition of some radical strangeness, inconvertible into *data* and resisting conceptualization and the knowing grasp (the *Auffassen* and the *Fassen*) that paves the way for the idealist besiegement of being by thought. These fields are irreducible because, while included within the relative order of the known world (that is, within the order amenable, in principle, to the phenomenological reduction), they belong to the noetic context, the fabric, the very flesh of the *I think* and its absoluteness. That belonging of the *I think* "to the flesh" is not a metaphor for Merleau-Ponty. The perception of things in their objectivity implies, noetically, and independently of any psycho-physiological preoccupation (of causality or conditionality), a movement of the sense organs and even of the hands and legs and the entire body: everything that is called life of the body as one's own body, as flesh incarnating thought; flesh that lets itself be identified by the subject with his or her body perceived *objectively*, as it is given to medical examination and to investigation by the psycho-physiological psychologist, and is thus a part of the mechanism of nature. Flesh then, as objective body, is thus constituted for consciousness out of "powers" that are already tributary to this body. Consciousness turns out to have already called upon what it is only just supposed to be constituting. An odd anachronism!

An anachronism consisting precisely in incarnation, in which the belonging of mind to body–which, as body, the mind constitutes–cannot be reduced to the noetic-noematic correlation, to pure theory. Is this the disqualification of the transcendental reduction, shown to involve an inevitable methodological contradiction, a kind of transcendental illusion? Is it the total failure of the wisdom of the return to self? Merleau-Ponty thinks that, for Husserl himself, the transcendental reduction was the unavoidable philosophical itinerary leading toward a realm of intelligibility that was not, obviously, that of the objectification sought by positive science, but one even more primordial than transcendental subjectivity.

The original incarnation of thought, which cannot be expressed in terms of objectification, and which Husserl may have still been suggesting in *Ideen I*, with the term "apperception," is prior, in Merleau-Ponty's view, to the taking up of any theoretical or practical position. An *Urdoxa*: a synthesis prior to all syntheses, "older" than the theses to which one might want to try to reduce it by setting out from a reasonable will or an intellectual activity of the postulated *I think*, and making a synthesis between *res extensa* and *res cogitans*.

Flesh. Flesh, which is called my body [*corps propre*], flesh which appears also as a body among bodies, but which, in those circumstances, is no longer approached in its concreteness, nor on its own terms. It is available to biology, which treats it as a thematizable object, as *Körper* rather than *Leiblichkeit*. This is not a shift toward a wrong meaning, but certainly toward an already abstract one. My own body, life. It is *here*, that is, at a point in space, but, being at this spot, a point of origin for a sentiency, a "point of view." A localization of that feeling that Descartes included, in the "Second Metaphysical Meditation," under acts included in the *cogito*, and not as *res extensa*. A body proper existing as lodging for a world, whose surroundings are not immediately "pure things," nor things clothed in "value attributes" linked to axiological intentions, already noetic-noematic in structure. The purely theoretical knowledge in which those things exist in that manner, and from which the noetic-noematic model of intentionality is doubtless borrowed, is a possibility, but already a derivative one, of that life. "There is undoubtedly something between transcendent Nature, naturalism's being in-itself, and the immanence of mind, its acts, and its noemata," writes Merleau-Ponty in *Signs*.[2] An in-between, more primordial than either!

Thus, according to Merleau-Ponty, who, with extreme perspicacity, returns to the exegesis of many texts from *Ideen II* (which the founder of phenomenology had never made up his mind to publish, however, and which appeared posthumously, thanks to the Husserl Archives at Louvain), Husserl's descriptions dropped the style of the transcendental philosophy proclaimed in 1913 in *Ideen I*. It is difficult for me to find terms adequate to express my admiration for the subtle beauty of the analyses in Merleau-Ponty's work of that original incarnation of mind [*esprit*] in which Nature reveals its meaning in movements of the human body that are essentially signifying, i.e. expressive, i.e. cultural; from gesture to language, to art, to poetry and science: that original incarnation in which Nature reveals its meaning (or its soul?) in Culture. The French philosopher's own quest doubtless permitted him to say the non-said (or at least the non-published) of Husserl's thought, a thought whose "possibilities" require an attentive ear throughout, despite the apparent immobility or restating of the main theses.

It is in sensibility, according to Merleau-Ponty, that the carnal (or the mental) manifests its ambiguity or its ambivalence of extension and interiority, and in which the *felt* [*senti*] that is there before us is *ipso facto* a *feeling* [*sentir*]. The sensible content is itself inseparable from that incarnation, of which it is the "reflection" or "counterpart," according to Merleau-Ponty. "A universe with its 'subject' and 'object,' without parallel, the articulation of one with the other."[3] The articulation of a subject with an object, in which one no longer finds the intentional structure of the noetic-noematic, an articulation Merleau-Ponty approaches by bringing to our attention what is called the double touching of one hand touching the other and that, during this touching, is touched by the other hand. The overall phenomenon is structured as if the touch were a reflection on touching; as if, according to a speculative expression of the philosopher's, "space itself knows itself through my body."[4] Here the human is only a moment or an articulation of an event of intelligibility, the heart of which is no longer enveloped or situated within the human being. Note must be taken of this anti-humanist or non-humanist tendency to link the human to an ontology of anonymous being. It is a tendency characterizing an entire era that, while reflecting upon anthropology, is suspicious of the human. The propounded doctrine would seem all the more defensible for appearing indifferent to the drama of persons. One might also wonder whether, to a certain extent, Merleau-Ponty is not rehabilitating in this instance, while deepening it, the sensualist conception of sensation which was at once a feeling and a being felt, without empiricism's having had to be alarmed by this psychism, which it understood as devoid of the dynamism of horizons and intentionality. The latter did not even reach beyond the pure "sensible quality," not even in cases where the object broke away, in a sense, from carnal experience, putting itself at a distance, and thus becoming distinct from feeling [*sentir*].

For Merleau-Ponty, the passage of sensible qualities bound to carnal subjectivity toward the condition of objective qualities of the real was thereafter sought in intersubjective agreement on this sensible content. That presupposes the constitution of intersubjectivity. Merleau-Ponty accentuates in *Ideen II* everything that makes the relation with others depend upon that carnal structure of sensibility. The way the two hands touch one another remains the prototype, so to speak, of that relation. "My right hand," Merleau-Ponty writes, "was present at the advent of active touching in my left hand: it is not otherwise that the body of the other comes to life before me when I shake another man's hand or when I just look at it."[5] The discovery of the felt [*senti*] as feeling [*sentant*] extends to the other's body without having given rise to a reasoning by analogy. The other person and I "are like the elements of one sole intercorporeity":[6] the co-presence of two hands, due to their belonging to the same body, has been extended to the other person. The "esthesiological" community is seen as founding intersubjectivity and serving as a basis for the intropathy of intellectual communication, which is not directly given, and is produced by reconstruction. This is not taken as an indication of any deficiency in our perception of others, but as the positive characteristic of that perception: "I borrow myself from the other; I make him out of my own thoughts: that is not a failure in the perception of others, it is the perception of others."[7]

We must ask ourselves, however, whether this way of affirming a positivity in what, at first blush and from a certain point of view, presents itself as privation, does not require the indication of a new dimension that would accredit that positivity. Is the insufficiency of "appresentation"[8] compared to representation in the relation with others no more than the consequence of finitude? Is it not the premise of a new relation between myself and others that is not just a deficient knowledge of them? Is it really nothing but knowledge? The latter remains in Merleau-Ponty–despite the originality of the pretheoretical structure he demonstrates, precisely as pretheoretical–already related to the theoretical and already as it were the shadow of that to which it is related. Even though it stands out in contrast to the noetic-noematic structure of idealizations, it is for

Merleau-Ponty–already or still–knowledge, though in a different mode. "Even with respect to things," he says, "we know much more of them in the natural attitude than the theoretical attitude can tell us about them–and above all we know it otherwise."[9] Intersubjectivity, constituting itself in sensibility described on the basis of the "reflected touching" of the hands touching one another, is structured according to the community between the "touching" and the "being touched," "the common act of feeling and being felt." It is a community that is affirmed in its agreement about [*autour de*] being–about things and the world. In the phenomenological theory of intersubjectivity it is always the *knowledge* of the alter ego that breaks egological isolation. Even the values the alter ego takes on, and those attributed to it, are based on a prior knowledge. The idea that a sensibility could reach the other *otherwise* than by the "gnosis" of touching, or seeing (though the seeing is visual and the touching a contact of the flesh) seems foreign to the analyses of the phenomenologists. The psychism is consciousness, and in the word "consciousness" [*conscience*] the radical "science" [*science*] remains essential, primordial. Thus, sociality does not break the order of consciousness any more than does knowledge [*savoir*], which, cleaving to the *known* [*su*], immediately coincides with whatever might have been foreign to it.

Whence a question. In the handshake that phenomenology attempts to understand on the basis of mutual knowledge [*connaissance*] (even if it be the case of the double touching), does not the essential, going beyond knowledge, reside in confidence, devotion and peace (and with an element of the gift, going from myself to the other, and a certain indifference toward compensations in reciprocity and thus with ethical gratuitousness), which the handshake initiates and means, instead of being a simple code transmitting information about it? Nor is the caress that bespeaks love the mere message and symbol of love, but rather, prior to that language, already that love itself. Hence one may in particular wonder whether such a "relation" (the ethical relation) does not impose itself through a *radical separation* between the two hands, which in point of fact do not belong to the same body, nor to a hypothetical or only metaphorical intercorporeity. It is that radical separation, and the entire ethical order of sociality, that appears to me to be *signified* in the nakedness of the face illuminating the human visage, but also in the expressivity of the other person's whole sensible being, even in the hand one shakes.

Beginning with the face–in which the other is approached according to his or her ineradicable difference in ethical responsibility–sociality, as the human possibility of approaching the other, the absolutely other, is signified [*signifiée*]–that is, commanded.[10] It is a possibility that does not borrow its excellence from the dignity of the *One*, with respect to which sociality may already appear, in its multiplicity, a degradation of sorts–but is rather a completely new modality attesting, in and through the human, its own *goodness*. In its excellence, which is probably that of love, the laws of being and its unity do not simply continue to rule. The spirituality of the social would seem to signify precisely an "otherwise than being."

Does the distinction, still current in everyday parlance, between matter and spirit, have a meaning any less naive today? Are not the numerous variations on the theme of the Aristotelian distinction between matter and form, virtuality and action, or on that of Cartesian dualism rendered doubtful (over and above the simplifications due to progress in the natural sciences and certain paradigms in the human sciences, and in addition to the speculations of transcendental idealism) by the realism of sociopolitical doctrines or by the challenging of subjectivity by modern philosophical anthropology, in which, in the principle of a meaningfulness [*du sensé*] "more original than the subject," the abyss between *res extensa* and *res cogitans* disappears? In this note I have asked whether the distinction should continue to be sought within some intrinsic structure of matter and spirit understood as essences constitutive of the world and as interconnected by the unity of the world. Perhaps the spiritual only shows, only reveals its specificity when being's routine is interrupted: in the strangeness of humans vis-à-vis one another, but of humans capable of a sociality in which the bond is no longer the integration of parts in a whole. Perhaps the spiritual bond lies in the non-in-difference of persons toward one another that is also called love, but that does not absorb the difference of strangeness and is possible only on the basis of a spoken word [*parole*] or order coming, through the human face, from most high outside the world.

9 In Memory of Alphonse de Waelhens

A paper on a point of general philosophy, which I shall read to you and which will take as starting point and pretext a thesis of Merleau-Ponty, will be my way of evoking the presence of the philosopher Alphonse de Waelhens, who was also my friend. I do not wish (after what has been said here, and all that has been written by the colleagues, friends and disciples of the deceased in memory of Alphonse de Waelhens in *Qu'est-ce que l'homme?*, published by Facultés Universitaires de Saint-Louis de Bruxelles)–I do not wish to repeat what has been so well said about the person and work which remain so much alive among us. But the general problem I want to address–in homage to the man who, in 1951, wrote the magnificent book on Merleau-Ponty entitled *Une philosophie de l'ambiguïté* [A Philosophy of Ambiguity]–arose from within the intellectual world in which de Waelhens lived during the entire first half of his philosophical life. And no doubt he would not have been indifferent to a homage that harks back to the years when what is called the philosophy of existence was in the forefront of intellectual life in France and Belgium, and when his name came up so often, along with those of Jean-Paul Sartre, Maurice Merleau-Ponty and Jean Wahl. De Waelhens was actively involved in that whole world, of which one of the most intense focal points was the Collège Philosophique, founded and led by Jean Wahl in Paris, just after the war. There, alongside the Sorbonne, in opposition to or in agreement with that institution at which Jean Wahl was, after all, a professor, philosophy opened itself to new sounds. It was there that the first echoes of *Being and Time* were heard, there that the influence of Edmund Husserl was confirmed. His works were already being disseminated with a renewed vigor, thanks to my eminent and fondly remembered friend, Father Herman van Breda, in the very place where we are gathered today. Alphonse de Waelhens would have enjoyed the recollection of that period, and it is a pleasure for me also to pronounce–articulating with affection–the venerable names of the dear departed of those times, as I commemorate his name.

But before moving on to the purely theoretical theme I promised to develop in memory of Alphonse de Waelhens, I would like to say a few words about the constant traits in the personality of that man whom I knew since his youth, before the Second World War. I had my first conversations with him a few years after the 1930 publication of my early work, *The Theory of Intuition in Husserl's Phenomenology*. Our early years were almost contemporaneous, separated only by my six years of seniority. Though our days together were spread out over time, that time extended over nearly half a century. It depended on geography: my trips to Belgium and his to Paris. Our meetings in Rome at the International Colloquia of Religious Philosophy, directed for years, early every January, by Professor Enrico Castelli, were for me among the highlights of those famous philosophical dialogues. I would like to bear witness to that friendship that was faithful and reliable, generous and frank. It was confirmed again in 1981 in Berne, Switzerland, where, a few weeks before he died, we found ourselves together among the five foreign philosophers whom, each year, the university of the Swiss capital brings in from abroad, inviting them to speak before its professors and students. Madame de Waelhens, whom I remember with warmth, was with her husband. (She followed him to the grave, as you know, a few weeks after his death.) In Berne I found an Alphonse de Waelhens already ailing, but no less faithful in his friendship, in his search for truth no less *severe*, no less demanding in his thought, which required reasons to *back up* the propositions one advanced, no less adverse to apologetics than during his entire life of teaching and research; whatever may have been his convictions and the secret of his beliefs, which were refractory to any exhibition and no doubt jealously held in private.

His talk at Berne, like many of his contributions over the years, such as his book on *Psychosis* [*La Psychose*] in 1971, or his very last work on *The Duke of Saint-Simon*, showed the prime importance Freudianism had taken on for him, after his entire youth and a large part of his adult life devoted to phenomenology and the philosophy of existence. *La philosophie et les expériences naturelles*, published in 1961, foreshadowed that new direction of philosophical interests. Already in his *Philosophie de l'ambiguïté* on Merleau-Ponty, published ten years earlier, we read, on page 146, of his concern with finding "what is philosophically valid in a theory such as Freudianism," although alongside the credit given Freud for "letting it be thought that a man's sexual life is a certain expression of himself," de Waelhens did not hesitate to condemn what, according to him at the time, was (in his expression) "perfect nonsense," in Freudianism.

Psychoanalysis never was, for de Waelhens, an empirical method, piling up observations with a view to some sort of generality to be proclaimed a psychological *law*. It was in the prolongation of Freud by Lacan, for whom, along with Freud, he had an admiration possibly equaling his youthful adulation of Heidegger and Merleau-Ponty. Psychoanalysis was basic research on the human spirit, possessing a permanent speculative loftiness, but in which the misery of the human condition and the sick man's suffering are no longer hidden from the speculative eye.

I often wondered, during my acquaintance with Alphonse de Waelhens, how it was he went from phenomenology to psychoanalysis, from the study of renowned texts to the questioning of patients in insane asylums, from modern philosophy, which, despite its startling innovation, settled easily into academic routine and remained *right-thinking*, to psycho-analysis, which, even when it won the day, never lost a hint of scandal. I think the transition reflects a deeper upheaval than a simple intellectual evolution. It is proof of de Waelhens's deep humanity. He used to speak in fact of his sudden discovery of the gap between the mental realm attended to by the philosopher, and the concrete drama of mental illness. Without rejecting essential ideas that probably reveal themselves initially far from the real, there is a *need to get down to the facts more closely*, in which those ideas are, at first, unrecognizable, but in which they are elucidated and justified by all the concreteness of human suffering.

The tortuous journey of the human. Perhaps the echo of the sound of his footsteps will also be audible in the notes on sensibility that I shall read to you in memory of Alphonse de Waelhens. They are the product of some reflections on Husserl and Merleau-Ponty, two philosophers our late friend admired greatly. Notes in which the intelligibility of ideas and knowledge becomes akin to affectivity signifying the proximity of one's fellow man.

On Sensibility

In "The Philosopher and His Shadow"[1] Merleau-Ponty suggests, citing Husserl's *Ideen II*,[2] that the *transcendental reduction*, a procedure that inaugurates phenomenology, was not, for its creator, solely a method for making possible the perception of the reality of the world constituting itself, without remainder, in a noetic-noematic correlation of intentionality. The *reduction* was also supposed to circumscribe, or bring to light, the *irreducible*. The irreducible could only be avoided in the "constitution" of the things of the world called "pure things," or "just things" (*bloße Sachen*), given exclusively to vision and hearing as pure representation; and, no doubt, before the objects of the world are marked by "value" attributes, before appearing as "utensils" or cultural objects, which would imply a reference to the "incarnation" of conscience, and before bearing a relation to other persons.

The irreducible in question does not derive in this case (the opinion of the "realist" philosophers notwithstanding) from the permanence, in the "world to be reduced," of some radical *difference* eluding the relation: resisting the intentionality of consciousness, the grasp of *conceptualizing*, of *taking up* inherent in the concept; a difference refractory to *being given*, positing itself as an absolute, and, in its alterity, "too strong," so to speak, for thought, and thus foiling all transcendental idealism.[3] It is a question of something entirely different! The irreducible circumscribed here does not come from a non-interiorizable outside, an absolute transcendence. In constituting consciousness itself, in the psychic content of the "I think" and its "intentions," a paradoxical ambiguity appears: the texture of the *constituting* is stitched with threads coming also from the *constituted*, without that provenance having had to answer to any "intentional aim." These *threads* belong to the psychic fabric, and, so to speak, to the very *flesh* of the spirit. This is not to be taken as a simple metaphor. The mental "gait" [*"démarche"*] of thought, for example, is also in the proper sense of the term the walk [*marche*] and movement of the human body; of a body moving on its legs to circumambulate the thing to be known, bending and straightening up to increase and improve the views of the real to be obtained: views ever unilateral, to be confirmed or challenged and completed by one another; movements of hands and fingers touching, head changing its vantage point of sight and hearing; movements of contraction and decontraction of the eye muscles. These muscular acts and acts of perception are "mixed," bound to the exploratory activity of a skin that touches. They are lived as "sensations," in which, as in the doctrine of empiricist sensualism, the *feeling* coincides, without any intentionality, with the *felt*.

These sensations are, like all feeling, according to Descartes, included within the broad notion of the *cogito*, and yet, they are already localizable and, through kinesthetic sensations, signifying movement. They are thoughts already extended, so to speak, and immediately superimposable onto the bodily regions of the feeling, thinking subject, onto the objective movements of his or her organs and muscles, in which the flesh also appears as a quasi-external thing, constituted, in its various parts, for the look, and, on all its surfaces, for the touch; just as much as a simple stone, in a noetic-noematic process of consciousness such as Husserl describes it for the "just things," placed (in his words) *facing* the "pure I." There is an ambiguity of the *mental* and the *extended,* characteristic of "physical" pain and pleasure, which are always localizable, characteristic of coenesthesia, in the general sensibility of corporeal *presence,* which is precisely the sensation of the spatial *here.*

Here we have thought lived as extension and not just, as in the transcendental model, as the *idea* of extension: extension belonging to the "flesh of a thought, to thought having a flesh." Extension is no longer the intentional correlative of thought, however interfused it may please us to imagine it. There is thus, in the transcendental reduction of sensibility, the manifestation of a vicious circle or an anachronism: that of a constitution presupposing—or already giving itself—the constituted. In that insistence of *Ideen II* on what Husserl calls *conditioning* of the conscious by "one's own body," there seems to be a return upstream to the phenomenological sources of the psycho-physiological doctrine in psychology. That return is justified through the reduction. It is a return that does not yet imply any naturalistic prejudice, even though it may, in the natural attitude, be expressed in causal terms and foster a confusion between conditioning and causality. In the "natural attitude" prior to the reduction, that return announces and founds the psycho-physiological method, once the phenomenological evidence of "conditioning" is linked with or prolonged by empirical information on the connection between the psychic and the peripheral and central nervous systems.

Might not sensibility, that conditioning of the mental in the lived body, that "incarnation" of thought described phenomeno-logically in *Ideen II*, be the effect, in the Husserlian "system," of a certain earlier *apperception* spoken of in *Ideen I*[4] and that might be understood as an original transcendental synthesis carried out by the *I think*-an assemblage, as it were, into a noetic-noematic representation, of that *I think* itself with *extension*, by that already constructed *I think*?

But Merleau-Ponty has already accustomed us to the idea that the lived body or living flesh is an original mode of being, irreducible to the simple synthesis of pure nature-*res extensa*-with the "I think"-*res cogitans*. "There is undoubtedly," he writes in "The Philosopher and his Shadow," "something between transcendent Nature, naturalism's being in-itself, and the immanence of mind, its acts and noemata."[5] It is something whose ontology is inscribed in sensibility, and in which the relation of thought to extension is, in its irreducibility, the *inhabiting* of a world, an *incolere*, the inaugural event of a culture. In sensibility, the relation between the *I* and the *other* of the world is not to be thought of as the assimilation of the world by the constituting act, but as *expression* of an inner in an outer, life as culture: the truth of knowledge would be, in this scheme of things, neither more nor less than a particular mode of culture. Culture does not come along and add extra axiological attributes, which are already secondary and grounded, onto a prior, grounding representation of the thing. The cultural is essentially embodied thought expressing itself, the very life of flesh manifesting its soul-original significance of the meaningful or the intelligible. It is a modality of meaning older than that of the dualistic metaphysics in Cartesianism or in the subject-object correlation blossoming into transcendental philosophy. The subject-object correlation is a derivative notion, presupposing, in particular, intersubjective agreement, which cultural forms require in order to signify being and world, and which truth requires in order to signify objectivity within being and world. This agreement is established, according to Merleau-Ponty, on the basis of flesh itself, on the basis of embodied spirituality, and of the sensible, which, in other persons, reappears as "a flesh of one's flesh," just as a right hand, touching a left (its "felt") touches it *ipso facto* as a "feeling" hand, feeling the hand that touches it. Herein resides the principle of *intropathy*, of the *Einfühlung* of which German psychology speaks and to which Husserl's phenomenology is related. By virtue of the fact that my right hand which touches my left touches a "feeling" entity, undergoing "kinesthetic and tactile sensations" like those undergone by my right hand, I lend to the hand of *the other* that I shake–the felt hand–immediately tactile and kinesthetic sensations of a feeling being. I lend them to him in this very contact such as I felt them in my left hand touched by my right hand. And this, without recourse to any reasoning by analogy whatsoever! I pass from my hand to that of the other as if both belonged to the same body. This loan, in the form of esthesiological transfer–is fundamental: it forms the basis of the reconstruction for me of the thought of the other, using my thought as point of departure. And Merleau-Ponty writes: "I borrow myself from others; I create others from my own thoughts. This is no failure to perceive others, it is the perception of others."[6]

It is not our intent to cast doubts, in Merleau-Ponty's remarkable analysis, upon the opening up of a path toward the recognition of other people in the "I borrow myself from others." But can the social unity toward which it claims to move be conceived solely on the basis of an intercorporeity understood as the solidarity of an organism in its *esthetic* unity? Is the meaning of intersubjectivity at the level of sociality attained so long as it remains understood on the model of the unity connecting the two hands of a man, "the right hand knowing what the left is doing"? Is the handshake a "taking cognizance," and a sort of coinciding of two thoughts in the mutual knowledge of one by the other? Is it not in the *difference*, proximity to one's neighbor? In a difference that, as proximity, can be reduced neither to an attenuated difference, nor to a partially abortive coincidence or assimilation, but a difference that (and this gives a new meaning to peace) is borne not by the psychism of intentionality and thematization, nor by the communication of information–but by the non-in-difference of responsibility-for-the-other; by *sentiment*, which, originally, is not the "intending of values," but *peace*, making a break in apperception-consciousness? Is the handshake not, then, an *attuning* of oneself to the other, a giving of oneself to him or her? To be sure, all sentiment is not love, but all sentiment presupposes or inverts love. The handshake is not simply the notification of that agreement, but before that notification the extra-ordinary event of that peace itself, just as the caress, awakening within the touch, is already affection and not information about sentiment.

Moreover, how can a relation of knowledge in which the perceived is neither seized nor found within the object, but only lent to it, mean anything but the failure of perception's very intentions, even if that knowledge is only a "knowing otherwise," according to Merleau-Ponty's own expression?[7]

Husserl's texts on *intropathy*, which were published in *Ideen II*, present the meaning of this *"knowledge"* in a manner that is indeed particularly impressive in its phenomenological preciseness. These analyses, many years earlier than those of the fifth meditation in Husserl's *Cartesian Meditations*, seem to me, paradoxically, richer than the latter. Specifically, I have in mind the whole of paragraph 56 of this dense but so very rich volume–and even more specifically the inimitable pages (236–247) on the understanding of objects "invested with spirit" (contrasted with our knowledge of all other meaningful objects): cultural and written ones. I have in mind the admirable effort to bring out, through the phenomenological analysis of appresentation, sociality and society in their height and preeminence in relation to the perception of objects simply endowed with "signification." Yet at no point in the course of that very beautiful analysis is the (ultimately or originally) cognitive structure of the lived put in question, in order to conceive of the cognitive accession to the objectivity of the other person on the basis of his or her proximity as neighbor, rather than founding the latter on the former. To the end, sentiment continues to be conceived on the basis of a knowledge of values.

It would be appropriate, in my judgment, to ask at this point whether–beyond, or on the hither side of an acquired or even immediate knowledge concerning the existence of a thought outside my own, revealing the fact of there being "someone to talk to" out there–entropathy itself is not already a fully social relation. Does it not, expressed by Husserl in the personal form of the reflexive verb, "*Ich fühle mich ein*," already resonate like a sympathy, a friendship and almost a kind of brotherly compassion, that is, a taking upon oneself of the "undergoing" ["*subir*"] of the other person? Its excellence in intersubjectivity is measured, not by the adequation of the perceived with the real, but by the generosity of the "I borrow myself from others," by the ethical value of the gift, of the lending of the loan agreed to from myself to the other, higher than the investing of being in pure knowledge. "To borrow oneself from others" is not of the order of esthesiological constitution. It is a "first move" granted to the other! To borrow oneself, the very metaphor of sociality insinuating itself into *contact*, ambiguous from the start. Sociality born of the signifying power of sentiment, already dulled in the purely qualitative and neutral sensation of the touch, and always on the verge of slipping back into it. Intersubjectivity is not the modality of a *sensation* in which, in the example of two hands touching one another–in the "double touching" as it was once called in psychology–pure knowledge would culminate. This is the case even if, in the ambiguity of the insinuation (the modality of the enigmatic or the "vacillating" [*"clignotant"*], and not simply the equivocal) there always remains the possibility of an un-saying [*dédire*] that nevertheless does not justify the reduction pure and simple.[8]

There is clearly in Husserl's analyses in *Ideen II*, on which many of Merleau-Ponty's are based, a priority given to the tactile, the kinesthetic, localizable pain and pleasure, in comparison with the other modes of the sensible; and in the reflections on touch and physical affectivity, there is an insistence that sensation, as knowing, should signify both as movement and as extension. Hence perhaps a certain priority granted to the ambiguity of the sensible as a form of consciousness in which the mental element of the apprehension of things and the spatial element of the corporeal gestures of taking, in that very apprehension, go together. Original (in both senses of the word) condition of the lived body, status of *Leiblichkeit,* of solipsistic subjectivity, and, in the other person, of the object "invested with spirit." But henceforth there is a priority granted to the flesh affirming itself in human spirituality, to the detriment of another ambiguity or ambivalence: that of the enigma of sensation-sentiment that is formed in the passivity of the senses affected by the sensory, between the pure undergoing or passive experience and eventual suffering, and the *known* of knowledge which remains as residue or trace. Pure undergoing, eventual suffering–solitude and abandonment as the concreteness of suffering. Solitude and abandonment, but thus, in the "privation" of the desire for the other, this desire itself. Affectivity bearing affection or love–secret structure or concreteness of sentiment. Should we say a waiting for God in this presentiment of the absolutely other? Not immediately nor at first an appeal for help, but a pathway leading to the other, which leads to the human. In the touch itself, the possibility of a helping hand. Or the possibility of the caress, the kiss, and the erotic.

The other, who, to affection, is unique, and who, through that uniqueness, is no longer a simple individual among individuals, grouped within a genus common to them, the unique who is precisely other to all generality, is bound to me socially. That person cannot be represented or given to knowledge in his or her uniqueness, because there is no science but of generality. But the non-representable–is it not precisely the inner, which, *appresented,*[9] is approachable? Appresentation is not only the last resort of a deficient representation, as certain of Husserl's texts sometimes lead one to understand. It is, in proximity, all the novelty of the social; proximity to the other, who, refusing to be owned, falls to my responsibility, that is, signifies in all the ethical excellence of the obligation toward the other, in fear for him or her, and love.

There is a lack of recognition or forgetting also, in Husserl and Merleau-Ponty, of the even more mysterious enigma of sensation-sentiment in the visual, which, as *unveiling par excellence*, as fully theoretical opening on *being*, as the synthetic, mastering grasp of it, englobes and totalizes universally, beyond the open horizons of the given–seizes and conceptualizes more being than hands could carry off. But behold how in this universal investiture there lies coiled the dispossession of dis-inter-estment beneath the concreteness of responsibility, of non-in-difference, of love. There is responsibility for the unique, shattering the totality: responsibility before the unique that rebels against every category, a signifier outside the concept, free, for an instant, from all graspable form in the *nakedness* of his or her exposure to death, pure appresentation or expression in his or her supreme precariousness and in the imperative that calls out to me. Behold vision turning back into non-vision, into insinuation of a face, into the refutation of vision within sight's center, into that of which vision, already assuming a plastic form, is but forgetfulness and re-presentation.

10 The Rights of Man and the Rights of the Other

1 The Original Right

The rights claimed under the title rights of man, in the rigorous and almost technical sense which that expression has taken on since the eighteenth century–the right to respect for the human dignity of the individual, the rights to life, liberty, and equality before the law for all men–are based on an original sense of the right, or the sense of an original right. And this is the case, independently of the chronology of the causes, the psychological and social processes and the contingent variations of the rise of these rights to the light of thought. For today's way of thinking, these rights are more legitimate than any legislation, more just than any justification. They are probably, however complex their application to legal phenomena may be, the measure of all law and, no doubt, of its ethics. The rights of man are, in any case, one of the law's latent principles, whose voice–sometimes loud, sometimes muffled by reality's necessities, sometimes interrupting and shattering them–can be heard throughout history, ever since the first stirrings of consciousness, ever since Mankind.

These rights are, in a sense, *a priori*: independent of any power that would be the original share of each human being in the blind distribution of nature's energy and society's influence, but also independent of the merits the human individual may have acquired by his or her efforts and even virtues. Prior to all entitlement: to all tradition, all jurisprudence, all granting of privileges, awards or titles, all consecration by a will abusively claiming the name of reason. Or is it perhaps the case that its *a priori* may signify an ineluctable authority, older and higher than the one already split into will and reason and that imposes itself by an alternance of violence and truth; the authority that is, perhaps–but before all theology–*in* the respect for the rights of man itself, God's original coming to the mind of man.

These rights of man, that do not need to be conferred, are thus irrevocable and inalienable. Rights that, independently of any *conferral*, express the alterity or absolute of every person, the suspension of all *reference*: a violent tearing loose from the determining order of nature and the social structure in which each of us is obviously involved; an alterity of the *unique* and the incomparable, due to the belonging of each one to mankind, which, *ipso facto and paradoxically,* is annulled, precisely to leave each man *the only one* of his kind. A tearing loose and a suspension–or freedom–which is no mere abstraction. It marks the absolute identity of the person, that is, of the non-interchangeable, incomparable and unique. A uniqueness beyond the individuality of multiple individuals within their kind. A uniqueness not because of any distinctive sign that would serve as a specific or individuating difference. A unity prior to any distinctive sign, a uniqueness logically indiscernible from the first person. A uniqueness that is not forgotten, beneath all the constraints of Being, History, and the logical forms that hold it in their grip. It remains concrete, precisely in the form of the various rights of man, claimed unconditionally, under the various necessities of the real, as various modes of freedom. Later I shall discuss the phenomenology of these claims, the structure of the consciousness in which they take shape concretely.

The rights of man manifest the uniqueness or the absolute of the person, despite his or her subsumption under the category of the human species, or because of that subsumption. This is the paradox, or mystery, or novelty of the human in being, which I have just stressed. It seems to me to be suggested by a remarkable talmudic apologue, which I quote:

> Grandeur of the Holy-Blessed-Be-He: Behold man, who strikes coins with the same die and gets coins all alike; but behold the King of kings, the Holy-Blessed-Be-He, who strikes all men with the die of Adam and not one is the same as another. That is why each is obliged to say: The world was created for me![1]

The fact that the identity of species can include the absolutely dissimilar, a multiplicity of non-additive, unique beings–that the unity of Adam marks the individuals of incomparable uniqueness in which the common species disappears and in which the individuals cease being interchangeable like coins–that they affirm themselves to be, each one, the sole purpose of the world (or the sole one responsible for the real): surely this is the trace of God in man, or, more precisely, the point in reality at which the idea of God comes only to man. This is a possible meaning of that apologue, which is not the equivalent of some deduction of the rights of man on the basis of a prior Revelation, but means, on the contrary, the coming of the idea of God on the basis of the patency of the rights of man.

That the rights of man or respect for those rights *does not proceed* from the sternness or the grace of God, as the latter are expressed in theologies appealing to Revelation, that is, to "truths about God" already acquired elsewhere (an appeal that would still bear witness to the extra-ordinary aspect of those rights, recognized as super-natural, but also already to the jurisprudence and mediation of the religious authorities)–*that* has been, since the Renaissance, the trait that has characterized the consciousness of the rights of man.

2 The Broad Notion of the Rights of Man

The possibility of ensuring the actual enjoyment of these rights–of making the facts respond to the unconditional claim to human freedom and all the rights therein implied, despite the weight of physical and political necessity, and even despite the violence in which the person may experience the pure *undergoing* of the things of the world–this possibility is not immediately given. The conditions for the respect of these rights are only apparent once man has already assumed his first right, in becoming aware of the natural and social determinism that hampers the person, and once, consequently, he catches sight of the practical procedures, issuing from that *knowledge*, capable of freeing the person from these pressures and of subordinating them to the exercise of his rights.

The taking up of one's freedom from within knowledge is not an inevitable fact for the humanity of all eras and all lands. A taking up of freedom which is itself free! That is a revolutionary act in the most radical sense of the term. It is the mark of an era and a civilization, an event of the Western world! Science and the possibilities of technology are the first conditions for the factual implementation of the respect for the rights of man. *Technical development thanks to the flourishing of theoretical knowledge* [savoir] *through which European humanity passed on its way toward its modernity is probably, in itself, the essential modality in which the idea of the rights of man, placed at the center of self-awareness, broadened in its conception and was inscribed or required as the basis of all human legislation; which legislation at least thought of itself as being the rights of man in their indispensable or hoped-for entirety.* A rational discipline, born in Europe, could broaden out and be available to all humanity. Into a world that until then was felt to be doomed to an arbitrary play of forces that (natural or supposedly supernatural, individual and social) only counted in proportion to their power, in the obstinacy that Beings and institutions invest in persevering in their being and their traditions–there came the *a priori* of the rights of man understood as intellectual *a priori*, and becoming in fact the measure of all law. Since the Renaissance, the actual laws regulating society began to be judged in reference to so-called "natural" law, which, as we know, means the latter's belonging to the order of truths bearing intelligibility and evidence and deriving, one way or another, from a consciousness of the rights of man. Need I recall the works of such men as Hugo Grotius and Puffendorf, in the seventeenth century, who developed the idea of law based on considerations similar to those of mathematics? The mind was thought capable of working from its own foundation, from its "innate" ideas, to undertake and carry out the construction of the Realm of Law. A law that would be valid independently of all tradition, indifferent to the empirical data of accepted laws. To other thinkers, the legal givens themselves seemed to make possible the formulation of these fundamental rights by induction, after a fashion. Montesquieu reduced the diversity of positive laws to determined principles, and brought out the spirit of those laws and their systematic interdependence.

Henceforth there would be attached to the notion of the rights of man–inseparably, and in ever-increasing numbers–all the legal rules that are the necessary conditions for the actual exercise of those rights. Behind the rights to life and security, to the free disposal of one's goods and the equality of all men before the law, to freedom of thought and its expression, to education and participation in political power–there are all the other rights that extend these, or make them concretely possible: the right to health, happiness, work, rest, a place to live, freedom of movement, and so on. But also, beyond all that, the right to oppose exploitation by capital (the right to unionize) and even the right to social advancement; the right (utopian or Messianic) to the refinement of the human condition, the right to ideology as well as the right to fight for the full rights of man, and the right to ensure the necessary political conditions for that struggle. The modern conception of the rights of man surely extends that far! True, it is also necessary to ascertain the urgency, order and hierarchy of these various rights, and to enquire as to whether they may not compromise the fundamental rights, when all is required unreflectively. But that is not to recognize any limitation to the defense of these rights; it is not to oppose them, but to pose a new problem in connection with an unquestionable right, and, without pessimism, to devote necessary reflection to it.

Thus the dynamic and ever-growing fullness of the rights of man appears inseparable from the very recognition of what are called the fundamental rights of man, from their requirement of transcendence, in a sense, of the inhuman that may be contained in pure nature, and of blind necessity in the social body. The uniqueness and irreducibility of human persons are respected and concretely affirmed by the diminishing of the violence to which they are exposed in the order, or disorder, of the determinism of the real.

But the development of science and technology which are supposed to make possible the actual respect for the enlarged rights of man may, in turn, bring with it inhuman requirements that make up a new determinism, threatening the free movements that it was to make possible. For example, in a totally industrialized society or in a totalitarian society—which are precisely the results of supposedly perfected social techniques—the rights of man are compromised by the very practices for which they supplied the motivation. Mechanization and enslavement! And this is the case even before adducing the banal theme of the necessary connection between technical advances, the development of destructive armaments, and the abusive manipulation of societies and souls. Whence a dialectic that could be too easily led toward the challenging or the condemning of technology, without any hope of a possibility of equilibrium, an eventual turning back of science and technology upon themselves. These are problems that cannot go undiscussed, for it is not only a new development of the rights of man in "civilized" countries that depends upon technical progress, but also respect for the elementary rights of man in the "third" and "fourth" worlds, threatened by disease and hunger.

3 The Rights of the Other Man

But do not the rights of man (that is, individual freedom, the uniqueness of the person) also run the risk of being belied or

infringed upon by the rights of the other man? What Kant calls
"a kingdom of ends" is a plurality of free wills united by reason.
But is the freedom of one not, for another's will, the latter's
possible negation, and thus at least a limitation? Is it not a
principle of possible war between multiple freedoms, or a
conflict between reasonable wills that must be resolved by
justice? A just legality, in agreement with universal laws, would
in Kant's view be obtainable through the resolution of a plurality
of opposing wills. And, indeed, through or with the rigor of
justice being imposed upon the "incomparable uniqueness" of
free persons, we witness the miraculous birth, a birth "out of
suffering," of the objective spirit of truth. But that justice
represents nonetheless a certain limitation of rights and free will.
Is it so certain that the entire will is *practical reason* in the
Kantian sense? Does the will not contain an incoercible part that
cannot be obligated by the formalism of universality? And we
might even wonder whether, Kant notwithstanding, that
incoercible spontaneity, which bears witness both to the
multiplicity of humans and the uniqueness of persons, is not
already pathology and sensibility and "ill will." There also
remains the question of determining whether the limitation of
rights by justice is not already a way of treating the person as an
object by submitting him or her (the unique, the incomparable)
to comparison, to thought, to being placed on the famous scales
of justice, and thus to calculation. Whence the essential
harshness of a law that offends, within the will, a dignity other
than that which attaches to respect for universal laws. The
dignity of goodness itself! The universality of the maxim of
action according to which the will is assimilated to *practical
reason* may not correspond to the totality of good will.

    Thus limited by justice, does not the fundamental principle of
the rights of man remain repressed, and does not the peace it
inaugurates among men remain uncertain and ever precarious? A
bad peace. Better, indeed, than a good war! But yet an abstract
peace, seeking stability in the powers of the state, in politics,

which ensures obedience to the law by force. Hence recourse of justice to politics, to its strategies and clever dealings: the rational order being attained at the price of necessities peculiar to the state, caught up in it. Necessities constituting a determinism as rigorous as that of nature indifferent to man, even though justice–the right of man's free will and its agreement with the free will of the other–may have, at the start, served as an end or pretext for the political necessities. An end soon unrecognized in the deviations imposed by the practicalities of the state, soon lost in the deployment of means brought to bear. And in the eventuality of a totalitarian state, man is repressed and a mockery made of the rights of man, and the promise of an ultimate return to the rights of man is postponed indefinitely.

This also means (and it is important that this be emphasized) that the defense of the rights of man corresponds to a vocation *outside* the state, disposing, in a political society, of a kind of extra-territoriality, like that of prophecy in the face of the political powers of the Old Testament, a vigilance totally different from political intelligence, a lucidity not limited to yielding before the formalism of universality, but upholding justice itself in its limitations. The capacity to guarantee that extra-territoriality and that independence defines the liberal state and describes the modality according to which the conjunction of politics and ethics is intrinsically possible.

But, given these considerations, in defending the rights of man, the latter should no longer be considered exclusively from the point of view of a conception of freedom that would already be the potential negation of every other freedom and in which, among freedoms, the just arrangement could only come from reciprocal limitation. Concession and compromise! The justice that is not to be circumvented requires a different "authority" than that of the harmonious relations established between wills that are initially opposed and opposable. These harmonious relations must be agreed upon by free wills on the basis of a prior peace that is not purely and simply non-aggression, but has, so to speak, its own positivity. Its dis-interestment is suggested by the idea of goodness, a dis-interestment emerging from love, for which the *unique* and *absolutely other* can only mean their meaning in the loved one and in oneself. To limit oneself, in the matter of justice, to the norm of pure measure, or moderation, between mutually exclusive terms, would be to revert to assimilating the relations between members of the human race to the relation between individuals of logical extension, signifying between one another nothing but negation, additions or indifference. In humanity, from one individual to another, there is established a *proximity* that does not take its meaning from the spatial metaphor of the extension of a concept. Immediately, one and the other is one *facing* the other. It is myself *for* the other. The essence of the reasonable being in man designates not only the advent in things of a psychism in the form of knowledge, in the form of *consciousness* rejecting contradiction, that would encompass the other things under concepts, disalienating them within the identity of the universal: it also designates the ability of the individual, who initially appears to exist relatively to the extension of a concept–the species man, to posit himself as *the only one of his kind*, and thus as absolutely different from all the others, but, in that difference, and without reconstituting the logical concept from which the *I* disengaged itself, to be non-in-different to the other. Non-in-difference, or original sociality–goodness; peace, or the wish for peace, benediction; "*shalom*"[2]–the initial event of meeting. Difference–a non-in-difference in which the other–though absolutely other, "more other," so to speak, than are the individuals with respect to one another within the "same species" from which the *I* has freed itself–in which the other "regards" me, not in order to "perceive" me, but in "concerning me," in "mattering to me as someone for whom I am answerable." The other, who–*in this sense*–"regards" me, is the face.[3]

This is a goodness in peace, which is also the exercise of a freedom, and in which the *I* frees itself from its "return to self," from its auto-affirmation, from its egotism of a being persevering in its being, *to answer for the other*, precisely to defend the rights of the other man. Non-indifference and goodness of responsibility: these are not neutral, midway between love and hostility. They must be conceived on the basis of the meeting, in which the *wish for peace*–or goodness–is the first language.

Should not the fraternity that is in the motto of the republic be discerned in the prior non-indifference of one for the other, in that original goodness in which freedom is embedded, and in which the justice of the rights of man takes on an immutable significance and stability, better than those guaranteed by the state? A freedom in fraternity, in which the responsibility of one-for-the-other is affirmed, and through which the rights of man manifest themselves *concretely* to consciousness as the rights of the other, for which I am answerable. Their original manifestation as rights of the other person and as duty for an *I*, as my fraternal duty–that is the phenomenology of the rights of man. But in their original *mise-en-scène* there is also the affirmation, as a manifestation of freedom, of the rights of the obligated person, not only as the result of a simple transference and thanks to a generalization of the rights of man as they appear in others to the obligated person. One's duty regarding the other who makes appeal to one's responsibility is an investing of one's own freedom. In responsibility, which is, as such, irrecusable and non-transferable, I am instituted as non-interchangeable: I am chosen as unique and incomparable. My freedom and my rights, before manifesting themselves in my opposition to the freedom and rights of the other person, will manifest themselves precisely in the form of responsibility, in human fraternity. An inexhaustible responsibility: for with the other our accounts are never settled.

11 The Strings and the Wood: On the Jewish Reading of the Bible

1

There can be no denying that the critical exegesis of the Holy Scriptures has had an unsettling effect upon religious minds.

Perhaps it signifies no more than the end of a simplistic conception of inspiration, the "death" of a god lingering in the "hinter-worlds," and (for all His having been the Supreme Power, the most just one, the only one worthy of our adoration) still acting as a force among forces, whose collaboration men hope for in war and love, and whose blessing is awaited as a recompense. It may even be that a less naive conception of the inspired Word than the one expiring beneath critical pens allows the true message to come through widely scattered human witnesses, but all miraculously confluent in the Book. Perhaps it is not because of scientific rationalism's penetrating Scripture that men have ceased hearing the Word; perhaps quite to the contrary, biblical criticism is gaining possession of the texts because of a listening that is incapable of perceiving the divine resonance of the Word, which, thus reduced to a linguistic fabric, itself requires the precautions of a science.

All this is possible–even probable. All this seems to me to be the case. But how to forget the strange authenticity of the no longer believable schema? Persons and communities who are crossing the deserts of Crisis unaffected by it–and who keep the Inheritance whole and intact–reassure our overly subtle minds. Their *credo* is closed to history, science and the infinite resources of Metaphor–but open to the high virtues and most mysterious secrets of Proximity.

2

But can the essence of Scripture be separated from the History and destiny of its readers, from their way of perceiving the Signs, from the meaning their reading retains by predilection? Must not tradition be seen in this case, not as guaranteeing the purity of the sources and fidelity of the transmission, but as a "place" wherein all the harmonics of the *said* resonate, wherein an entire life is breathed into the letters of the text, inspiring it? Do not these inspirations, though they may be authenticated by the continuity of their succession, hark back to others that enigmatically preceded them? All the way back to the text itself, overdetermined by the "ancient newness" of *the commentaries*? A text stretched over a tradition like the strings on the wood of a violin! Scripture has a *mode of being* distinct from that of pure matter available to the grammarian's analysis. A being such that the history preceding writing counts less than the lessons following it; such that inspiration is measured by what it has inspired; such that a break is produced in the synchronic system of signs circulating within immanence so that, under cover of the first signified, other significations begin to make themselves heard, calling for a new Saying, an interpretation: these are some of the traits of an ontology that the scientific thematization of the text cannot but miss.

These observations are valid for many religious traditions. But they are particularly pertinent to the Jewish one, because of the exceptional ties between Israel and the Bible, because of its way of welcoming Signs, and its predominant interest in the ethical and social side of biblical teaching, to the detriment of the theology and theosophy it may contain.

The Jews, at least in the Western world, were partially the promoters of biblical criticism. Spinoza's *Theologico-Political Treatise* had initiated the genre by the end of the seventeenth century. In nineteenth-century Germany a *Wissenschaft des Judentums* [Science of Judaism] thrived, prolonged in France in a worthy manner by the *Revue des Études juives* [Journal of Jewish Studies]. None can doubt the value of the efforts and talents brought to bear, the results obtained and promised, the conscientiousness of the scholars, whose reputation (often justified) for objectivity and intelligence was established by their refusal to take the path of apologetics and homily. But the lucid labors of that science have never been able, to this day, to take the place of that other reading, which is neither the private domain of the so-called "orthodox" circles, nor the stylized daily practice of the underdeveloped classes.

3

The fact that the Old Testament or Sacred History of the Christian West is, for the most part, the ancient history of a contemporary people, despite its dispersion among the nations or its integration with those nations, doubtless constitutes the originality of this people, its religious life and its reading of the Bible–or at least the memories it retains of that life and that reading.

In opposition to the transfiguration into myth (whether by degradation or sublimation) that threatens this "profound past," there stands the astonishing reality of today's Jews, few though they are in number and constantly diminished by persecution–weakened by indifference, temptations and apostasy.

As a defense against "mythologizing," a current concern, these traits also characterize the liturgy, which remains, objectively, the reality of Judaism, despite all the denials in which there is sometimes more snobbery than free thinking. At once commemoration of Sacred History and a continuation of the events commemorated, the practices are, through *interpretation,* reinserted into the texture of those events. It is quite remarkable, for instance, that the celebration of Passover, in which much emphasis is placed on the story of the exodus from Egypt (there is a vying for who can tell the most about it; a narrative heavily laden with symbols, and the internalizing of which takes place spontaneously, in a sense), ends with a commentary specially directed to the ritual acts of that night that are connected to the Flight from Egypt: the eating of the unleavened bread and bitter herbs. In this way the narrative loses its archeological character, and the ritual gestures lose their appearance of ordeals. And once the rite has been explained, there appears in the Ritual of the Feast the text in which Celebration becomes actualization, a personal reenactment of the past that has just been evoked:

> In each generation, each one must consider himself or herself as having gone out of Egypt personally .... It is not just our ancestors whom the Holy-One-Blessed-Be-He brought out of Egypt, but ourselves; he delivered us with them.

To belong to a book as one belongs to one's history! This explains how, in the name of the Book and in the perspective opened up by it, an historical act can be accomplished as a ritual gesture. The turning back to a land claimed as ancestral and promised may offer the most accurate view of the inner status of Scripture. It is situated beyond the space in which any philology can unsettle it.

4

The Bible–a volume inhabited by a people. But also a volume that has nourished that people, almost in the literal sense of the term, like the prophet who, in Ezekiel 3, swallows a scroll. A singular digestion of celestial food! In the Jewish reading, episodes, figures, teachings, words, letters, receive–through the immediate meaning, as if it were transparent–other innumerable meanings. Parable and homily (genres known by philologists but which appear minor to them) have stored the treasures of

Jewish thought and spirituality. Their diversity, their very contradictions, far from compromising the truths commented upon, are felt to be faithful to the Real, refractory to the System.

The Talmud and its commentaries, and the commentaries on these commentaries, collections of apologues, all the genres of "rabbinical literature," prolong (while stabilizing in writing) a very ancient oral tradition from which the Bible emerged and in which, for a Jew, it breathes. There is not a verse, not a word in the Old Testament that did not open out onto that world enveloping the readable! "Rabbi Akiba interpreted down to the very ornaments of the letters." These scribes, these doctors, who are called slaves of the letter, tore loose from those letters all the spirit to which they awakened the mind. "God said it once, I heard it twice. . . ." This fragment of verse 12 of Psalm 62 proclaims that innumerable meanings reside in the Word of God–if we are to believe the Rabbi, who, in the spirit of this pluralism, scrutinizes the very verse that propounds it.

Long before the "historical method," the rabbinical dialectic had destabilized verses, words and letters. It would of course be absurd to deny the existence within Judaism of a theology and a *credo*; they bear little resemblance, however, in their style, to a dogmatics. The doctors of the Talmud did not formulate them as a system or a synthesis. The metaphysics that can be extracted from their apologues, parables and legal lucubrations consists entirely of discussion and dialogue. Only the formulation of the practical precepts of law, morals and rites takes the form of statutes. Must one not admit that the presence of that Bible within the pluri-dimensional space opened up by its verses, interpreted in keeping with the pluralism claimed for the Word of God, distances it from the Old Testament as torn to pieces by historians who, in the process, have torn one another to pieces? The vessel of Scripture, afloat in the immense ocean of rabbinical dialectic, can hardly be endangered by the squalls of a few philologists who do not even know the vessel's draught.

In any case it is by plunging into that hitherto forgotten sea that an entire generation of young Western Jewish intellectuals thinks of itself as belonging, in matters of exegesis, to the post-critical age. "I am post-critical," as Martin Buber, too, used to say.

5

In Judaism, preoccupied with behavior, action and rites, the practical orientation which consists in reading the Bible through the Talmud (the relation with God being always mediated by one's neighbor and by the defense of "the poor, the widow, the orphan, the stranger") makes it possible for those [Jews] who think of themselves as belonging to the "post-critical" period to answer the attacks of modern anti-humanism when it accuses a spirituality made up of "beautiful souls and belles-lettres" of indifference to true human suffering. A thoughtful examination of that book of "pure spirituality," the Psalms, in the light of rabbinical texts borrowed for the occasion (which will make our earlier remarks more concrete) will serve as our conclusion.

The Psalms of David are the prayers of Israel. They have become the liturgy of the nations. They trace out, in our space, the way leading from the most intimate interiority–to beyond all exteriority. A fourth dimension, permanently opened up in the torn space of Europe and of the entire West. A singular way, taken (without knowing its name, itinerary or destination) by both the scholar's quest and the poet's attention, both the long patience of the oppressed and a revolutionary impatience; but a way opened by humble religious daring, a thankfulness giving thanks for its own thankfulness, a language that has managed to call upon the Nameless.

To seek a presence–absolute–at the center of a silence, to despair in the heart of hope, but to quench one's thirst with the very infinity of its fire, to proclaim that beneath the protection of an Invisible Pastor I shall not want: religious adventure, paradox and lyricism find in the Psalms their expression and model.

And yet, for Jewish thought, this book is also one of

teachings. "For Jewish thought": by that I mean the thought of the doctors and scribes who lived approximately between the second century B.C.E. and the fifth century C.E., and whose understanding of these 150 chapters (which date back to remote antiquity) determines the emotion of "the Jew of the Psalms," if indeed any still exist in the modern world.

What is immediately striking is the intimate bond between the keenest religious sentiment and the Law. "I am a stranger on the earth; Hide not Thy commandments from me," says Psalm 119: 19. The Law as joy, consolation, deliverance. Never the Law as a yoke! That will probably astonish Christians. But from among the many aspects the Psalms offer to Jewish sensibility, I wish to dwell upon a meaning that responds to the crisis that everyone's religious consciousness is undergoing today.

Certainties amidst uncertainty, or uncertainties amidst certainty, troubling the soul in its serenity, or its shell–that whole dramatic inner dialogue, nourished no doubt by the Psalms–do these not emphasize our leaving the world, a retreat, and, consequently perhaps our insensitivity to its misery, its hunger, its tears? Are we not in a situation I found myself in recently? A meeting of a high intellectual level, called to discuss some fundamental concepts of our Western spirituality, was held in a room in which we began to hear the shouts of protest of a crowd of students who were probably demonstrating against something entirely unrelated to the meeting we were holding. But the entire meeting became caught up in it. The religious order set above the ethical–the extreme tension of the direct relation with the Totally Other–the presence and the dissimulation of God–Kierkegaardian themes in which religious consciousness, in its noble form of today, expiates the peaceful conformism of the preceding period: have not these themes in turn become ambiguous? An ambiguity perhaps avoided by the rabbinical reading of the Psalms, often forgotten even by contemporary Jews. We read on page 7a of the Tractate Sanhedrin: Rabbi Samuel bar Nahmani said in the name of Rabbi Jonathan: Every judge who judges according to the truth causes the Divine

Presence–the Shekinah–to descend upon Israel, for it has been said, Psalm 82: 1, "God standeth in the congregation of God; In the midst of the judges He judgeth." And any judge who does not judge according to justice causes the departure of the divine presence, the Shekinah of Israel, for it has been said (in reference to Psalm 12: 6) "Before the oppression of the humble, the sighing of the poor, at that time I arise, saith the Lord." An arising to depart, without a doubt, in Rabbi Jonathan's opinion. But an arising that is also the revelation of the other face, of the angry face of God, the face of strict justice, announcing catastrophes and the overthrow of the established order: "I bring safety to the one whom they surround with snares," says the end of the verse just quoted. Presence and absence attained not by the mystic gifts of the soul, but by the just conduct of a tribunal. What a striking association of divine life with the institutions of the Republic!

But here is, in the same spirit and even more radically expressed, another meditation on the same verse (12: 6). In the collection of apologues, also very early, called *Bereshith Rabah* (section 75, para. 1) we read:

> Rabbi Pinhas has said in the name of Rabbi Reuben: Five times in the book of Psalms doth King David beseech the Holy-One-Blessed-Be-He to arise. Psalm 3: 8: "Arise, O Eternal One, come to my aid." Psalm 7: 7: "Arise, O Lord, in Thine anger, Lift up Thyself in indignation against mine adversaries, and, in my favor, exercise the justice Thou hast proclaimed." Psalm 9: 20: "Arise, O Lord, let not man prevail; Let the nations be judged in thy sight." Psalm 10: 12: "Arise, O Lord; O God, lift up Thy hand; Forget not the humble." Psalm 17: 13: "Arise, O Lord, forestall his designs, make him bend the knee; with Thy sword, save my life from the wicked."

But the Holy-One-Blessed-Be-He said to him: "David my son, even though you bid me arise so many times, I do not arise. And when do I arise? When you see" (this is a reference to Psalm 12: 6) "the poor oppressed and when you hear the sighs of the miserable—then will I arise, saith the Eternal One." Ah! Of course David the Psalmist remains the son of the Eternal One and the favorite son. But it is also as if his prayer, still, for whatever purpose it may be, the imploring of a serene soul—a soul shut up in its shell—were not equal to the task of attaining the sharp point of presence—the arising of God: as if that arising could only rightfully be beseeched in the suffering and sighs of the oppressed themselves, oppressed to the point of not knowing that they are praying to God with all their suffering—to the point of not knowing that, in the street they have come down into, they are also, unbeknownst to themselves, on the way that leads from the most inner intimacy to beyond all exteriority.

12 Everyday Language and Rhetoric without Eloquence

1

Rhetoric, as is well known, designates the art that is supposed to enable us to master language: whether it be, as Plato laments, to persuade the hearer by means of a discourse devoid of truth, showing the appearance of truth in verisimilitude, creating the illusion of truth; or whether it be, as Aristotle would have it, by seeking the conditions of a credible, persuasive discourse in the extension of the conditions of truth. Rhetoric thus includes the knowledge of certain "figures" of the *said*, of the circumstances in which they are appropriate and the rules for their effective use.

But it is also possible to understand by the term rhetoric these figures of discourse themselves, the structure that belongs to language. Already at the level of elementary analysis, discourse does not appear in the simplicity of a relation connecting, on a one-to-one basis, verbal signs and their corresponding realities. At the level of words, one constantly sees a distance between the things designated in an apparently natural way, on the one hand, and on the other the meanings that differ from them and that the words truly express; a distance between the "proper" meaning of the word and its "displaced" or metaphorical, figurative meaning. And it is as if this rhetorical movement of the "word in its literal sense" that carries it toward the figurative sense were not merely an effort to overcome an indigence of vocabulary and to designate a being or notion for which we have no words; it is as if the metaphor were necessary to the very signification it "produces" by its reaching beyond the literal meaning, which, in its own way, participates, lingering unforgettably, in the signification.

Which leads us to doubt whether thought begins with the reception of a datum by perception before language has formed it. The function of language would appear to be not just to express–faithfully or unfaithfully–a prior, totally internal thought: its rhetoric seems a part of the intellectual act, and to be the very intrigue in which a *this-as-that* is assembled; a this-as-that at the heart of a *datum* that, according to Heidegger's usage, would already be world; this-as-that, the paradigm or infrastructure of the metaphor in the broadest sense–of all resemblance, all metonymy, all synecdoche. A creative or poetic work rather than a simple association by resemblance, which would be conditioned by the former. But the talent of metaphor and rhetoric would appear to be already the gift of intelligence. We can assume and discover the displacement of an older meaning in the significance of every word. Not one would bear a literal meaning.

That hypothesis is all the more justified when we consider that, ultimately, words are always the beneficiaries of the meaning conferred upon them by their role in the semantic unit of the statement. They are, on one hand, a kind of abbreviation of multiple contexts; on the other, bearers of the trace of their etymology. Thus they signify as the very divergence between meanings. Here we must think of the resurgence of these truncated contexts, and of the reawakening in words of their dormant etymology. Let us recall the role played by these resurgences and especially by these reawakenings in the philosophy of a Heidegger. Does one reach a first meaning in this unfolding of meanings? It is in the distance between the senses of words that meaning means.

2

But if words literally have no proper meaning, they do possess a certain fixity of meaning within an order that, at first sight, can only be defined in a purely empirical manner: in daily life. Words at that level have a current meaning due to their usage surrounding interhuman relations based on custom and tradition and the everyday repetitions they entail. Those are the meanings of words according to usage, as if the language were nothing but a "tool." Indeed, but it is also a whole folklore of proverbial wisdom, thought and language being constituted in the proximity and familiarity of interlocutors who know each other. I shall come back to this idea.

One might legitimately wonder whether a certain referring back to "everyday language"–despite all the rhetoric that has already had a hand in elaborating it–is not to be recommended, as a precautionary measure made necessary by the freedom or poetic license of the metaphor. The latter may be introduced into a thought that is unrelated to the goals of poetry. The critical lessons given to thinkers, from Plato to Kant, must not be forgotten. Kant is the one who warned us about the false hopes of the dove who expects to fly more easily in a vacuum than in air. It is true that it took several hundred pages of his Transcendental Dialectic to convince us of it; more than a bird's brain could accommodate! But, since then, we know it does not suffice to be conscious of thinking to be certain one is really thinking.

There is certainly no question here, in this return to everyday language, of having the vernacular, as "truth," replace the less everyday language of speculation and poetry, in which rhetoric is less fixed, and in which metaphor, talent and invention are more alive. Nor is it a matter of having everyday language replace the algorithmic language of science, which, seemingly stripped of all rhetoric, is nonetheless indebted to the Cartesian metaphor of man as "master and possessor of nature." "This-as-that": that formal expression itself is not without context. One of the essential contributions of Husserlian phenomenology consists in having shown the necessity of pursuing the philosophical clarification of "formal" logic in the concreteness of "material" experience. To isolate the instances of metaphorical language's reference to everyday speech, to describe its modes of transcendence, is to carry out an operation similar to the one recommended by Husserl, inviting us in the *Krisis* to reduce the world conceived on the basis of science and culture to the "life-world." True, in Husserl, these meanings of the life-world, expressed in terms of everyday life, must be traced back to their constitution in transcendental consciousness, and be said in a discourse other than that of either daily life or the algorithm. And there also seems to have been in Husserl's thought an attempt–perhaps unavowed–to go back to a language on the hither side of all metaphor. It is probably difficult to separate language and rhetoric–which would constitute, for Husserl's quest for the absolute in the form of transcendental idealism, a major difficulty. Or does the philosophical genius consist precisely in the power of finding the first words, and do the great systems make up the foundation of our rhetoric? But the confrontation of the metaphorical with everyday language also reflects another concern: the protection of truth from eloquence. We must now reflect on this. It is by beginning with such reflection that a more rigorous definition of everyday language itself may be given, and that I will be able to bring its significance for philosophy to bear in a more precise manner.

3

Rhetoric is not only the discrepancy between a meaning and the everyday sense of a verbal sign, drawing its semantic effect from both the origin and the term of that discrepancy, effectively participating, through this interplay of signs, in the organization of experience and thought–and through its poetic effects, in catharsis, spiritual elevation or liturgy. Rhetoric brings into the meaning in which it culminates a certain beauty, a certain elevation, a certain nobility and an expressivity that imposes itself independently of its truth. Even more than verisimilitude, that beauty we call eloquence seduces the listener. Aristotle already emphasizes that embellishment and ennoblement through the metaphor. Those qualities were essential in situations where persuasion was the main thing, where the voters had to be convinced: before the tribunal, in the public square, in competitions, precisely those occasions for which the Sophists prepared their paying students. But these places of discourse, in ancient society, were kept separate from private life.

Clearly in our time the effects of eloquence are everywhere, dominating our entire lives. There is no need to go through the whole sociology of our industrialized society here. The media of information in all forms–written, spoken, visual–invade the home, keep people listening to an endless discourse, submit them to the seduction of a rhetoric that is only possible if it is eloquent and persuasive in portraying ideas and things too beautiful to be true. But now we immediately condemn eloquent discourse and suspect, beneath that florid literature, the presence of politics and propaganda, and "all the rest is literature." All the rest, i.e. the loftiest thoughts: religious, political and moral. We resort to everyday parlance to bring down and profane the heights of eloquence and the verbal sacredness it engenders. Even everyday speech is found to be not everyday enough, not straight enough. The decency of words, the noble cadence of oratorical speech, the respectability of books and libraries must be debunked. Bring in the filthy words, interjections, graffiti–make the walls of the city cry out.

Céline's *Journey to the End of the Night*, from which Sartre did not hesitate to excerpt an epigraph for his *Nausea*, may have been the signal launching that anti-literature that is one of the forms of what is called anti-humanism today, and one of the reasons for it. A language purposely crude that hopes to achieve straightforwardness in a certain vulgarity–but which previously appeared in "belles-lettres" only in the realist novel, for example, as local color–has become the proper mode of expression of the writer desirous, according to Verlaine's old precept, of "wringing the neck of eloquence."

This struggle against eloquence is carried out not only–as a form of terrorism–in our old, so-called capitalist West, which has been lulled for centuries by the eloquence of "belles-lettres," fine manners and dreams of impossible ideals. In those areas that consider themselves socialist, the eloquence of a certain sort of progressism would seem to have taken over even everyday speech. One must read Alexander Zinoviev's *The Yawning Heights* to witness the efforts of everyday speech to recover from the spell of that invasion. In that book it is as if, in order to regain one's lost sincerity, ordinary language were not enough, and had to be enhanced by words and phrases more negative and more destructive than negations. Hence the abundance, in that strange work, of a language that scoffs and pokes fun at itself: pages that sound like a radio broadcast purposely scrambled at the source. Hence also the deployment of the whole frightening and nihilistic arsenal of scatology: shouts, curses, obscene poems. But–and this may denote a strange powerlessness of language in its very power–the language directed against eloquence in turn becomes eloquence. Too beautiful to be true, does language not also become too horrible to reflect reality?

4

So what is everyday speech after all, in its shifting stability, whose meaning, despite its own rhetoric, remains a reference point for metaphors reaching beyond it over the entire span from the mathematical formula to poetry, and from obscenity to eloquence? There is a shifting stability of everyday speech, since in its purely functional, empirical usage, even when it remains a pure tool of practical communication, it varies with the culture of the speakers, their knowledge and their reading, their generation and social milieu. Already there is a certain element of eloquence involved in the use of everyday speech. But can we speak of the *essence* of everyday speech, and what is the distinctive trait of that essence?

To answer this question, we must again ask ourselves what the meaning of language is, such as we have viewed it up until now. In keeping with the great tradition of our philosophy, language is not the simple expression of a thought held to exist prior to it, to which it would conform; it is always seen as an order of phenomena destined to do the same work as that of thought: to know and to reveal being. Though it is not reducible to the inner psychic workings of thought, it nevertheless remains the locus of truth. It is in relation to truth that it is judged, and, in its rhetorical excesses, condemned by Plato as a source of illusion. In Hegel it is the element in which the dialectic is carried out. In Husserl–or at least in the early Husserl–surreption and drifting of meaning (*Sinnverschiebung*) take place in language, but the thought going toward being revealed "in flesh and blood" has an immediately logical structure. It will find its likeness in language.

In Heidegger, for whom the "language that speaks" is not subject to the hazards of human speech–for whom it is language that speaks in human speech (*die Sprache spricht*)–it is the revelation of being that coincides with that speaking. Hence the language of everyday life can only be a fallen language; it becomes *Gerede*, its own "object" and its own goal, conforming to what *they* say, what *they* do, what *they* read, motivated by a vain curiosity, comfortable with ambiguity. It has fallen from the ontological status of language, and appears to have no other subject than the anonymous "they," once it loses the horizon of the being of beings, the field of truth.

I wonder whether, in that whole tradition, language as *Said* has not been privileged, to the exclusion or minimizing of its dimension as *Saying*. There is, it is true, no Saying that is not the Saying of a *Said*. But does the *Saying* signify nothing but the *Said*? Should we not bring out, setting out from the *Saying*, an intrigue of meaning that is not reducible to the thematization and exposition of a *Said*, to that correlation in which the Saying would bring about the appearing of beings and being, "putting together" nouns and verbs into sentences, synchronizing them, in order to present a structure? The *Saying* signifies otherwise than by its function as an attendant![1] Beyond the thematization of the Said and of the content stated in the proposition, *apophansis* signifies as a modality of the approach to the other person. The proposition is proposed to the other person. The *Saying* is a drawing nigh to one's neighbor. And as long as the proposition is proposed to the other person, as long as the *Said* has not absorbed that approach, we are still within "everyday language." Or, more precisely, in everyday language we approach our fellow-man instead of forgetting him in the "enthusiasm" of eloquence.

In everyday language we approach the other person. The *Saying* is not exhausted in the giving of meaning as it inscribes itself–fable–in the Said. It is communication not reducible to the phenomenon of the *truth-that-unites*: it is a non-indifference to the other person, capable of ethical significance to which the statement itself of the Said is subordinate. The proximity that declares itself in this way is not a simple failure of the coinciding of minds that truth would bring with it. It is all the surplus of sociality. Sociality that is also irreducible to *knowledge* of the other; it is delineated in language after an entirely different model than intentionality, despite all the importance given to the *Said* in language and that is further emphasized in a rhetoric already departing from the everyday logos.

Doubtless the rhetoric of the *Said* can absorb the ethics of proximity; but it is to the degree that that proximity is maintained in discourse that the circle within which the "life-world" signifies is drawn, within which *everyday exchanges* take place, and from which eloquence is excluded under penalty of provoking laughter. It is not by the degree of elevation achieved by the inevitable rhetoric of all speech that the essence of the "life-world" and "everyday language" can be defined; the latter are described by proximity to one's neighbor, which is stronger than that rhetoric, and in relation to which rhetoric's effects are to be measured. But it is also in the proximity to the neighbor, remaining *totally other* in that proximity, that–beyond the *distantiation* of rhetoric–the significance of a *transcendence* is born, going from one person to the other, to which metaphors capable of signifying infinity bear reference.

13 The Transcendence of Words: On Michel Leiris's *Biffures*[1]

Surrealism's undertaking goes beyond the ambitions of a literary school. It consists in identifying metaphysical and poetic freedom. The capriciousness of the dream, in its very absurdity, does not proceed from a fatality that defeats the dignity of our personhood, but rather espouses the form of a liberation. It is not the privilege of genius. Non-sense is the most evenly distributed thing in the world. But in Breton's first manifesto there was a naive confidence in the clandestine and miraculous energies of the Unconscious; his references to Freud are like allusions to some mythological region, fertile in hidden treasures. And his critique of the conscious mechanisms of thought was less the result of an analysis of them than the anticipation of the impasses to which their use brings us.

Michel Leiris, who at one time belonged to the Surrealist group, also exalts (in his own way, it is true) that power of the dream in his most recent book, *Biffures*. But rather than availing himself of I know not what mystical power of the Unconscious, he finds causes for his dreams. Causes drawn from conscious life. The abundance and apparently unexpected quality of the images is due, first of all, to *associations of ideas*, whose "latent birth" Michel Leiris patiently describes.

Up until the middle of the book we witness a prodigious expansion of Rimbaud's famous sonnet.[2] But the correspondences evoked cease being mysterious. They are traced to their genesis. Michel Leiris is a chemist rather than an alchemist of the verb. From page 128 on, that chemistry extends to facts, situations and memories. It becomes the real content of the narrative, which is at once a work of art proposed as such and a reflection on the essence of that art. Which, after all, is quite in keeping with the tradition of French poetry from Mallarmé to Blanchot, in which the emotion that constitutes the matter of the work is the very emotion that formed that matter.

In the very last part of his work, Michel Leiris reveals the technique of his art to us: "*bifurs*" [bifurcations, or forks in the road] or "*biffures*" [crossing out, or deletions], which give the book its title, and a meaning to that astonishing rehabilitation of the association of ideas. Bifurcations–because sensations, words and memories invite thought to turn off, at every instant, from the direction it seems to have taken and to travel unexpected paths; crossing out–since the univocal meaning of these elements is, at every instant, corrected, written over. But in these bifurcations or crossings-out it is not so much a question of exploring the new paths opened, or of holding to the corrected meaning, as of seizing thought at the privileged moment at which it turns into something other than itself. It is because of that fundamental equivocation of the "*bifur*" that the very phenomenon of the association of ideas becomes possible.

Whereas we are in the habit of reducing the function of signifying to the association of ideas, accustomed to thinking that the multiplicity of meanings of the sign, verbal or other, is explained by the network of associations surrounding it–with the notion of the "*bifur*" the process of the association of ideas loses its fundamental role. Thought is originally "*biffure*" [crossing out], that is, symbol. And because thought is symbolic, ideas can fasten onto one another and form a network of associations. Hence, whether due to the circumstances in which the word was learned, or to its sounding similar to other words, or even to its written form, thus enriched by all that written signs in turn make one think of–this network has its value, not in its ability to facilitate the passage from one idea to others, but because it facilitates the presence of one idea in another. Just as the animals in a fable are not there solely to suggest a moral, but, by their physical presence they enrich the suggested idea, so thought, at the moment of its "*biffure*" [crossing out], still counts by its crossed out meaning; its different meanings participate in one another. Surrealist freedom is not opposed to the other mechanisms of thought: it is their supreme principle.

The association of ideas, grasped at the level of "*biffures,*" therefore becomes a thought beyond the classical categories of representation and identity. This overflowing of thought might remind one of Bergson's duration—but the Bergsonian conception consists in representing that negation of identity in the form of becoming. The originality of the notion of *biffure* comes down to positing the multiple as simultaneity, and the state of consciousness as irreducibly ambiguous. The memories of Michel Leiris, related according to his "rule of the game," do not leave you with the impression (and this is quite odd) of a temporal rhythm. The ambiguity of *biffures* forms rather a space.

It would be interesting to compare the technique of *biffures* to the work of modern painters. I recently saw some paintings by Charles Lapicque. Destroying perspective in its function as the order of walking and of approach, Lapicque creates a space that is mainly an order of simultaneity. This process is similar to a literary description, which achieves depiction not by reproducing the continuity of extension, but by assembling certain details in an order determined by the nature of those details, by their power of suggestion. It is not space that houses things, but things, by their deletion, that delineate space. The space of each object sheds its volume. From behind the rigid line there emerges the line as ambiguity. Lines rid themselves of their role as skeletons to become the infinity of possible paths of propinquity. Forms vary on their essential themes like the sea foam on which Charles Lapicque is working now, in which all sensible matter is reduced to those infinite suggestions of one form emerging from another. A variation on themes, but not musical, being without duration; precisely simultaneous and spatial. The very form of one sole picture would bring this play of obliteration to a halt. The painting, in Lapicque's work, is accompanied by variants that do not have the function of *studies* moving toward the *ne varietur* of the finished work, but are on the same footing with it. Incompletion, not completion, would seem, paradoxically, to be the fundamental category of modern art.

But does not the spatial aspect of this play of crossing out derive from its visual aspect? The proliferation of deletions is surely a kind of return of consciousness to its sensible existence, the return of the sensible to its sensible as sensible, to its esthetic essence. But the particular symbolism contained in the esthetic essence of reality–is it not to be explained by the specific nature of the visual experience to which Western civilization ultimately reduces all mental life? That experience involves ideas; it is light, it seeks the clarity of the self-evident. It ends up with the unveiled, the phenomenon. All is immanent to it.

Seeing is being in a world that is completely *here*, and self-sufficient. All vision beyond the datum remains within the datum. The infinity of space, like that of the signified to which the sign refers–is nonetheless of this world. Vision is a relation to being, such that the being attained by it appears precisely as world. Sound, in turn, offers itself to intuition, can be given. It is doubtless in this that the primacy of vision over the other sensations consists. It is upon this primacy of vision that the universality of art is based. It makes beauty in nature, calming it, appeasing it. All the arts, even the sonorous ones, create silence.

A silence at times of the bad conscience, oppressive or frightening. This need to enter into relation with someone, despite and above the achievement and the peace of the beautiful–I call it the need for critique.

There is in fact in sound–and in consciousness understood as hearing–a shattering of the always complete world of vision and art. Sound is all repercussion, outburst, scandal. While in vision a form espouses a content and soothes it, sound is like the sensible quality overflowing its limits, the incapacity of form to hold its content–a true rent in the fabric of the world–that by which the world that is *here* prolongs a dimension inconvertible into vision. It is thus that the sound is symbol *par excellence*–a reaching beyond the given. If, however, sound can appear as a phenomenon, as *here*, it is because its function of transcendence only asserts itself in the verbal sound. The sounds and noises of nature are words that disappoint us. To really hear a sound is to hear a word. Pure sound is the word.

Contemporary philosophy and sociology have accustomed us to undervalue the direct social relations between persons speaking, and to prefer the silence or the complex relations determined by the framework of civilization: mores, law, culture. A disdain for the word, derived no doubt from the degeneration that menaces language, from the possibility of its becoming idle chatter or empty formalities. But it is a disdain that cannot gainsay a situation whose privileged nature is revealed to Robinson Crusoe when, in the tropical splendor of nature, though he has maintained his ties with civilization through his use of utensils, his morality, and his calendar, he experiences in meeting Man Friday the greatest event of his insular life–in which a man who speaks replaces the ineffable sadness of echoes.

Which means, of course, that the social relation–the real presence of the other–matters. But which means more especially that that presence, far from signifying pure and simple coexistence with me, far from being explained by the romantic metaphor of "living presence," is fulfilled in hearing, and draws its meaning from this originally transcendent role played by the proffered word. It is to the extent that the verb refuses to become flesh that it ensures a presence among us. The presence of the Other is a presence that teaches; that is why the word as teaching is more than the experience of the real, and the master more than a midwife of minds. He wrenches experience away from its esthetic self-sufficiency, from its *here*, where it rests in peace. And by invoking it he transforms it into a creature. In this sense, as we have said elsewhere, critique, the spoken word of a living being speaking to a living being, leads the image, with which art was content, back to fully real being. The language of critique takes us out of our dreams, of which artistic language is an integral part. Clearly, in its written form, critique always attracts further critique. Books call for more books, but that proliferation of writing stops or culminates the moment the living word enters in, the moment critique flowers into teaching.

This privilege of the living word, destined to be heard, compared to the picturesque word-image or sign, also becomes apparent when the act of expression is examined.

Is self-expression only the manifestation of a thought by a sign? That notion is suggested by written texts: disfigured words, "frozen words,"[3] in which language is already transformed into documents and vestiges. The living word struggles against this turning of thought into vestige; it struggles with the letter that appears when there is no one to listen. Expression bears within itself the impossibility of in-itself being, of keeping one's thought "for oneself" and, consequently, the inadequacy of the position of the subject in which the ego disposes of a given world. To speak is to interrupt my existence as a subject, a master, but to interrupt it without offering myself as spectacle, leaving me simultaneously object and subject. My voice brings the element in which that dialectical situation is accomplished concretely. The subject who speaks does not place the world in relation to himself, nor place himself purely and simply at the heart of his own spectacle, as does the artist, but in relation to the Other. This privilege of the Other ceases being incomprehensible once we admit that the primary fact of existence is neither the *in itself*, nor the *for itself*, but the "*for the other*"; in other words, human existence is creature. By the proffered word, the subject that posits himself exposes himself and, in a way, prays.

In these remarks, too cursory for so grave a topic, the event of expression proper is situated outside its traditional subordination to thought. The conception according to which the word serves only to communicate thought (or to conceal it) is backed by

such an old and venerable tradition that one scarcely dares go
against it. I think Michel Leiris's crossings-out exhaust,
magnificently, all the possibilities of exploring thinking thought
[*la pensée pensante*] in contact with the sensible matter of words
themselves; but they still agree with the primacy of thought in
relation to language stated in the classic phrase "that which is
well conceived . . .".[4] The riches brought by language are not to
be assessed, in the final analysis, for Michel Leiris, otherwise
than by their counterpart in thought content.

14 Outside the Subject

1 From Subject to Object

Psychologism in logic–a product of late nineteenth-century naturalistic empiricism–attempted to reduce the ideality of the logical and mathematical forms of scientific thought, the thought of an intelligence, of a thinking I, to the psychological phenomenon–individual but anonymous–of thinking itself. Reduction of the *ideal* and of the *I* to a thinking that is not the thinking of an I–to anonymous thinking taking place in time and subjected to the laws, the empirical constants, that regulate the psychism's changes of state as manifested in the form of thought. Laws or constants visible to consciousness reflecting upon itself. Empirical psychological laws, more coercive than the intellectual act of an *I* who would think freely–an *I* that might be illusory within a universal determinism. Hence the temptation to reduce the universality and the ideality of ideas and concepts, as well as the unity of the "I think" (which not very long ago had seemed to dominate the *res cogitans* and the *res extensa*), to the order of nature and the anonymity of the particular (which, since Aristotle, is supposedly the "only thing that exists"), to the unfolding of mental reality, *to the subjective, which thus becomes the matrix of all the thinkable.*

Edmund Husserl's *Logical Investigations,* inaugurating phenomenology and already availing itself of it, questioned, from the beginning of the century, that naturalistic interpretation of consciousness and the reduction of thought to a psychological mechanism. Husserl not only showed the radical skepticism implied by that doctrine, which immediately compromised its own claim to truth; he insisted upon what was termed the *intentional* character of consciousness, thereby destroying the image of a monolithic consciousness and an interpretation of psychic phenomena according to a matter-based model. All consciousness is conscious of that consciousness itself, but also and especially of something other than itself, of its intentional correlate, of its *thought-of.* A thought [*pensée*] that is conscious of a thought-of [*pensé*], which, as object, is inherent in thought, without being cut from the same cloth, so to speak. An opening of thought onto something present to thought and quite distinct from the lived experience of that thought. Husserl stressed the irreducibility of intentionality: a being-open-to that is neither a principle of contiguity, resemblance or causality, nor one of a deducible consequence, nor yet again the relation of sign to signified or of the whole to the part. Intentionality–from thought to thought-of, from subjective to objective–is not the equivalent of any of those relations that can be read off the object or between objects. Openness of thought onto the thought-of. "Openness onto": a thinking that is not, however, a blind shiver [*frisson*] of the mental, but that, precisely as intention, is a project: "project" of a thought-of, which, though not cut out from the mental fabric of thought, is "unreally" inherent in it, and presents itself in thought as in-itself. It shows itself within–manifests itself in the in-itself or is in-itself in manifestation.

In opposition to the natural temporal flow of mental or subjective reality and the empirical constants in which psychologism sought an empirical rationality, Husserl's phenomenology, in its analysis of subjectivity, preserved the objectivity or the in-itself, or the presence, or the being of the object,

sheltering it from all confusion with the lived psychism of
thought; and it supported that objectivity in its independence,
by the invariable objectivity of logical, mathematical forms, and
by the rational necessity of the *eidetic*. Visible, and therefore true
forms. All consciousness is consciousness of something. Consciousness is not only the lived experience of the psychism, of
the cogitations assured of their subjective existence: it is
meaningfulness [*du sensé*], thoughts casting themselves toward
something that shows itself in them. For a whole generation of
students and readers of *Logical Investigations*, phenomenology,
heralding a new atmosphere in European philosophy, meant
mainly thought's access to being, a thought stripped of
subjectivist encumbrances, a return to ontology without criticist
problems, without relativism's fears–the flowering of the eidetic
sciences, the contemplation of essences, the method of the
disciplines named regional ontologies. Logic itself, enlarged to
form a *mathesis universalis* and entitled "formal ontology,"
invites subjective thought to espouse its forms. "The return to
the things themselves," the rallying cry of phenomenology, is
most often understood as that priority of being over the
consciousness in which it shows itself, dictating its Law to the
acts of consciousness and their synthesis.

2 From Object to Subject

And yet the ultimate lesson of Husserl's phenomenology–which distinguishes within the subjective, thanks to the
notion of intentionality, between the subjective of the lived
psychism and the objective that, through that subjective, is
projected or shows itself–does not consist in turning its back on
the element of that projection that is purely act, in order to lose
itself in the objective theme and thereby become worthy of
scientific dignity. Phenomenology does not want to be *naive
realism*. It tells us, according to Husserl, that thought absorbed
by the object is precisely naive; it teaches that, separated from its
intentional birth in consciousness, the objective remains an

abstraction exposed to inevitable misunderstandings, to be prevented by focusing on the emergence of the objective from the subjective. It should of course not be said, as the psychologists would have it, that the objective is always already subjective. But it should be said that the objective, separated from the subjective that carries it, or constitutes it "intentionally," is abstract, hiding its own perspectives, the work of a naive thought. Husserl's phenomenology tells us that the scientific or philosophical manner of understanding is to study the constitution of the objective articulations of being–things, values, correlates of affectivity and will–*in* the concreteness of thought and the noetic-noematic life of consciousness, cleared of all prior contamination by the prematurely affirmed objective–in a mode of thought, sought after or attained, called pure or transcendental consciousness, by an operation termed *phenomenological reduction*. An operation that brings out, in the phenomenon, all the dimensions of meaning, all the "horizons" that would escape the notice of a naive thought, one that neglected to reflect upon its own functioning. Naive thought: as if the thinking subject need not beware of what he or she can posit otherwise than by thinking, or as if, outside the thinking subject, there were still meaning.[1]

3 The Pure Ego

But what seems primordial in that transcendental phenomenology, stressing the concreteness of the phenomenon as noetic-noematic intentionality, is the origination of the "phenomenon" in what Husserl's *Ideas* introduced as early as 1913 under the name *pure ego* (and to which the 1901 *Logical Investigations* still objected as being a product of the influence of a lingering psychologism)–a notion to which great importance would henceforth attach. Phenomenology is not to be conceived of as the discourse of an anonymous psychism; the intention of noetic-noematic thought is the intention of an ego that is no more drawn "from the body" of the psychism of consciousness than is the object; an ego that, "transcendent in immanence," according to Husserl's paradoxical expression, remains unique, and, thus, absolute, unrelated to anything else, in itself, although living in actuality or actively in the acts of consciousness that "proceed from it." No reduction has any hold on it. . . . It is absolutely devoid of explicit components, an indescribable in-itself and for-itself, pure I and nothing further.[2]

The I, absolute and pure, to which the noetic-noematic life goes back and whence it springs, undergoes and doubtless withstands the supreme methodological test, the *Transcendental Reduction*, through which Husserl returns to thought, untainted by the "things of the world," which have only to "keep quiet," so to speak, to be and to appear, to show themselves plainly and directly without even the shadows that might be projected by them onto the pure and impassible Me or I. The ego remains untarnished, not worn or marked by phenomena, preserved from any unnoticed or secret commerce with the object, free of any premature complicity with the true, in a domain in which appearing [*l'apparaître*] is all that counts. Identity and impartiality of the pure I who does not subject unveiled being–the phenomenon, constituting itself or showing itself in the intentions–to the risk of being anachronistically enlisted, as soon as it appears, in the service of presuppositions. Identity of the pure I and possibility of a temporality in the phenomenon thanks to a subtle intentionality of *retentions* and *protentions* having entered into the initial presence of the proto-impression. Time related thus to its unique *exstasis* (which is rather *authority* [*instance*] of the present), authority that will return in *re-presentation*. A thought in which the being of beings will in the final analysis be *presence* in the synthetic truth of a theory. Identity of the I–identity of uniqueness already exempt from all membership that, as in the case of the simple individual, would have brought it to the promiscuity of individuals contained within the extension of a genus in which they are placed and are the equivalent of one another. Uniqueness, identity of uniqueness, precisely *me* or *I* who is not just a metaphor for the identical, but its original meaning in its self-awakening–an awakening to self that is not reflective consciousness, an awakening predestinating identity to transcendental purity. The transcendental I, who does not arise out of any thematizing operation and does not claim for itself the identity of the *same* that reveals itself in the diverse, in the name of a "common" difference. A logically unjustifiable identity, showing itself in the *I* of the said, in the saying [*dire*] that belongs in some way to the constitution of the I it expresses. Vigilance of a continual reawakening, *I* that, Rimbaud notwithstanding, is not an *other*. Identity of the *I*, protected from all surprise of an "already," from any *fait accompli* and outside all kinship. Identity of the unique, brilliantly named *monad* by Leibniz, unchanging identity–the wonder of which should astonish us more than it does.

4 A Subject Outside the Subject

We should be more astonished at that monadic identity, that identity of uniqueness in the *I* that has no need of justifying itself logically as the individuation of a kind by the addition of an attribute differing from the one possessed by other individuals of the same kind, or by an irreducible position of the individual in space and time–the famous material individuation. The *I* is different because of its uniqueness, not unique because of its difference.

What is the source of that uniqueness, which cannot be understood as the residue of an abstraction, of a return of the individual to the ideal unity of the kind, to which the individual belonged? Its meaning is certainly not constituted, in turn, in a subject more absolute, so to speak, than the constituted absolute, moment of the "bad infinity," moment of an iteration. The pure I, the subject of the transcendental consciousness in which the world is constituted, is itself *outside the subject*: *self* without reflection–uniqueness identifying itself as incessant awakening. It has been distinguished, ever since the *Critique of Pure Reason,* from any datum presented to knowledge in the *a priori* forms of experience, and "rational psychology" has even been condemned for having taken it as the sublime but legitimate object of knowledge. It is by setting out from the implications of the *Critique of Practical Reason* that the transcendental I will be postulated beyond its formative function for knowledge [*forme dans le connaître*]. And Husserl, in his critique of the Cartesian *cogito*, the reflective turn of which he admires, is critical of the fact that in Descartes' *Meditations* the *I* is uncovered and certain, at the horizon of the world. The *pure I*, which the Cartesian ego becomes in the *phenomenological reduction*, takes on, from that point on, the exceptional status of a transcendent I in the very immanence of intentionality, "indescribable pure Ego and nothing more."[3]

5 Before Truth

And nothing more? Objectivation, the projection of intentionality—are these the ultimate secret of thought that the phenomenological vocation of philosophy has to clarify? Does the light that is at the beginning of thought manifest itself only in the form of a light shining on the forms that bring together in presence, and allow one to think together, the chaotic thickness of the *hylē*, which Husserl's texts refuse to omit, even in their polemics against empiricist sensualism and the affirmation of intentionality? Is the light of thought destined only to help us see the synthetic forms that—through the jumbled content of the elements, the structureless elements of the sensible—have already tied (at the deepest possible level) the knot of simultaneity—the morphology of which it would then be phenomenology's calling to establish? It is no doubt because of that light, belonging to the intentional act, belonging to the noesis whose role it is to illuminate the forms of the noemata, modalities of the meaningful and rational—that Husserl's magnificent discovery of affective and axiological intentionality (without which the entire non-theoretical, lived experience of consciousness would lapse into "hyletic" content) contains the affirmation of a "doxic element that resides within all positionality."[4] This would also indicate, for the meaning of being, the priority of presence and representation, that is, simultaneity maintained in the guise of a theoretical system.

But the positing of the transcendental I in its absolute uniqueness, ensuring the truth of being in the realm of appearance–is it not ordered, in its uniqueness, in a different light than the one illuminating the structures of the phenomenon? Does it not hark back to the ethical intrigue prior to knowledge? Face to face with the other man that a man can indeed approach as presence, and that he does approach as such in the sciences of man, had not the thinking one [*le pensant*] already been exposed–beyond the presence of the other, plainly visible in the light–to the defenseless nakedness of the face, the lot or misery of the human? Had he not already been exposed to the misery of nakedness, but also to the loneliness of the face and hence to the categorical imperative of assuming responsibility for that misery? The Word of God in that misery committing him to a responsibility impossible to gainsay. A uniqueness of the irreplaceable and chosen. From unique to unique, beyond any kinship and any prior commonality of kind–a closeness and a transcendence outside all subject, outside all synthesis of a mediator. But an awakening to the indescribable "pure I" of transcendental constitution, recovered by the phenomenological reduction.

Notes

Translator's Introduction

1. "La conscience non intentionnelle," in the collection: C. Chalier and M. Abensour, eds., *Emmanuel Lévinas* (*Les Cahiers de l'Herne*) (Paris: Editions de l'Herne, 1991), p. 113. The translation (and all other non-attributed ones) is my own.

2. In the collection: J. Rolland, ed., *Emmanuel Lévinas* (*Les Cahiers de la Nuit Surveillée*, 3) (Lagrasse: Verdier, 1984), pp. 19–36.

3. The phrase is from Levinas's *De Dieu qui vient à l'idée* (Paris: Vrin, 1982): quoted by J. Colette in *Emmanuel Lévinas* (*L'Herne*), p. 23.

4. "Translator's Foreword," in *The Theory of Intuition in Husserl's Phenomenology* (Evanston: Northwestern University Press, 1973), pp. xi–xxviii.

5. "Levinas, Rosenzweig, and the Phenomenologies of Husserl and Heidegger," in *Philosophy Today*, 32 (1988), n. 2, pp. 165–178.

6. See pp. 100, and 114 [Fr. 150, 170], and *De Dieu qui vient à l'idée* (Paris: Vrin, 2nd ed. enl., 1986), p. 221.

7. See Richir's "Phénomène et Infini," in *Emmanuel Lévinas* (*L'Herne*), pp. 241–261, esp. pp. 244–245.

8. See *Philosophical Investigations*, ed. S. C. Rome and Beatrice K. Rome (New York: Rinehart & Winston, 1964), pp. 23–29.

9. In *The Provocation of Levinas: Rethinking the Other*, ed. R. Bernasconi and D. Wood (London and New York: Routledge, 1988), pp. 100–135.

10. In J. Derrida, *Writing and Difference*, trans. A. Bass (Chicago: Chicago University Press, 1978), pp. 86–151.

11. *Otherwise than Being or Beyond Essence*, trans. A. Lingis (The Hague: Martinus Nijhoff, 1981), p. 25. Quoted in *The Provocation of Levinas*, p. 129.

12. Originally delivered as a paper on September 27, 1959, at the second Colloquium of French-speaking Jewish Intellectuals, organized by the French section of the World Jewish Congress. Translated by Richard A. Cohen in *Midstream* (November 1983), pp. 33–40, but omitting the last five pages. Retranslated by Seán Hand, in *Difficult Freedom* (London: Athlone Press, 1990), pp. 181–201.

13. See Levinas's Introduction to Stéphane Mosès's *System and Revelation*, trans. C. Tihanyi (Detroit: Wayne State University Press, 1992).

14. Salomon Malka, *Lire Lévinas* (Paris: Les Editions du Cerf, 2nd ed., 1989), p. 105.

15. "Lévinas et Rosenzweig," in *Emmanuel Lévinas* (*Les Cahiers de la Nuit Surveillée*, 3), p. 52.

16. See Levinas's *Difficile liberté*, 3rd ed. (Paris: Albin Michel, 1963 and 1976), p. 254. In English, see *Difficult Freedom*, trans. Seán Hand, p. 182.

17. It is doubtless because of this desire to develop a philosophy more adequate to interpersonal relations and open to ethics that Levinas felt an affinity to Kant's practical reason. See Levinas's "L'ontologie est-elle fondamentale?" in *Entre nous: Essais sur le penser-à-l'autre* (Paris: Ed. Grasset & Fasquelle, 1991), pp. 13–24, esp. p. 23.

18. *Entre nous*, p. 10.

19. See David Banon's "Une Herméneutique de la sollicitation," in *Emmanuel Lévinas* (*Les Cahiers de la Nuit Surveillée*, 3), pp. 99–115, esp. p. 100.

20. *Entre nous*, p. 9. The biblical reference is: "The fear of the Lord is the beginning of wisdom."

21. See Catherine Chalier's *L'Alliance avec la nature* (Paris: Les Editions du Cerf, 1989), p. 79.

22. Merleau-Ponty, *Signs*, trans. R. C. McCleary (Evanston: Northwestern University Press, 1964).

1 Martin Buber's Thought and Contemporary Judaism

1. [*Translator's note*: Levinas is referring to two successive drafts of what was to become Pope Paul VI's "Nostra aetate," or "Declaration on the Relation of the Church to Non-Christian Religions," promulgated on October 28, 1965. The first schema (November 20, 1964) was considerably more liberal than the final draft.]

2. *Spinoza et l'interprétation de l'écriture* (Paris: Presses Universitaires de France, 1965). [*Translator's note:* Levinas wrote a commentary on this work entitled "Have You Reread Baruch?" Cf. Levinas's *Difficult Freedom*, trans. Seán Hand (London: Athlone Press, 1990), pp. 111–118.]

3. [*Translator's note*: A lecture by Gabriel Marcel preceded that by Levinas. The quotation referred to is the following. "The single man in *isolation* possesses in himself the *essence* of man neither as a *moral* nor as a *thinking* being. The *essence* of man is contained only in the community, in the *unity of man with man*–a unity, however, that rests on the *reality* of the *distinction* between 'I' and 'You.' From Feuerbach's *Principles of the Philosophy of the Future*, para. 59, in *The Fiery Brook: Selected Writings of Ludwig Feuerbach*, trans. and ed. Zawar Hanfi (Garden City: Doubleday, 1972), p. 244.]

4. [*Translator's note:* This criticism of Buber's Meeting (as being too "spiritual," too "ethereal") was also expressed in "Martin Buber and the Theory of Knowledge" which originally appeared in German in 1963 ("Martin Buber und die Erkenntnistheorie") in *Martin Buber, Philosophen des 20. Jahrhunderts*, and it elicited a response by Buber, to which Levinas responded by letter. The article itself has been translated in *The Levinas Reader*, ed. Seán Hand (Oxford: Blackwell, 1989), pp. 59–74, but not the dialogue it initiated. The latter appears partially in Levinas's *Noms propres* (Montpellier: Fata Morgana, 1976), pp. 44–48.]

5. [*Translator's note:* i.e. in the tradition of Maine de Biran (1766–1824).]

2 Martin Buber, Gabriel Marcel and Philosophy

1. See the collective work on Buber which appeared in German (1963) and then in English, under the title *The Philosophy of Martin*

Buber, ed. Paul A. Schilpp and Maurice Friedman (La Salle, Illinois: Open Court Publishing Co.; London: Cambridge University Press, 1967); read the article by Gabriel Marcel, p. 42.

2. Gabriel Marcel, *Metaphysical Journal*, trans. B. Wall (London: Rockliff, 1952), pp. 210–11. [*Translator's note*: Translation slightly altered.]

3. *The Philosophy of Martin Buber*, p. 41.

4. Besides the study published in *The Philosophy of Martin Buber*, there is another essay of Marcel's on Buber entitled "Anthropologie philosophique de Martin Buber," in the collection published in 1968 by Editions de l'Institut de Sociologie de l'Université Libre de Bruxelles: *Martin Buber. L'homme et le philosophe*, pp. 17–41. I will cite it by this last title.

5. *The Philosophy of Martin Buber*, p. 41.

6. Ibid., p. 45.

7. *Being and Having*, trans. K. Farrer (New York: Harper & Row, 1965), p. 11. [*Translator's note*: I have modified Farrer's translations slightly.]

8. Ibid., p. 14.

9. Ibid., p. 12.

10. Ibid., p. 14.

11. Ibid.

12. Ibid., p. 28.

13. Ibid., p. 10.

14. Ibid., p. 11.

15. Ibid., p. 28.

16. *Metaphysical Journal*, p. 137.

17. *The Philosophy of Martin Buber*, p. 44.

18. *Martin Buber. L'homme et le philosophe*, p. 19.

19. *The Philosophy of Martin Buber*, p. 45.

20. Ibid., pp. 45–46.

21. Ibid., p. 47.

22. Ibid., p. 46.

23. [*Translator's note:* In French, "*risque dés-inter-essé.*" Levinas nearly always hyphenates *dés-inter-essé* to bring out the Latin etymological meaning: "not-within-being." The overall sense of the expression would then seem to be: the risk of leaving "being" in the discursive address, which constitutes a leap toward the other.]

24. Is not Brentano's famous thesis, that every psychic phenom-

enon is either a representation or founded on a representation (a thesis that never ceased to preoccupy Husserl), refuted or at least contradicted by the I–Thou psychism, which requires no I–It for its foundation? See, on the contestation of the "autonomy" of the I–Thou, the very important book by Yochanan Bloch: *Die Aporie des Du. Probleme der Dialogik Martin Bubers* (Heidelberg: Lambert Schneider, 1977).

25. *Martin Buber. L'homme et le philosophe*, pp. 31–32.

26. Babylonian Talmud, Tractate Shevuot, p. 39a. An expression in which Israel is to be understood as shorthand for humanity.

27. Edmund Husserl, *The Crisis of European Sciences and Transcendental Phenomenology*, trans. David Carr (Evanston: Northwestern University Press, 1970), p. 253.

28. Ibid., p. 254.

29. Ibid., p. 255.

30. Ibid.

31. Ibid., p. 256.

32. Ibid., p. 258.

33. [*Translator's note:* This phrase echoes Pascal's "The heart has its reasons, that reason does not know."]

3 Apropos of Buber: Some Notes

1. [*Translator's note:* "I–Thou" is my translation of Levinas's "*Je–Tu*," which in turn is his translation of Buber's "*Ich–Du*." The French (and German) pronouns are those used familiarly, between friends or equals. Levinas questions their appropriateness to designate the relationship between self and other because (differing from Buber on this point) he considers the other to be higher and greater than the self, and the relation to be asymmetrical and non-reversible. In fact, the relation with the other (person) takes place in the "trace" of the relation of self to God. This latter is to be understood in terms of "illeity," i.e. as an "I–It" relationship, though it should not be confused with the one Buber and Marcel reject in favor of the "I–Thou" to describe the human encounter. See Levinas, *En découvrant l'existence avec Husserl et Heidegger* (Paris: Vrin, 2nd ed. enl., 1988), p. 202.]

2. [*Translator's note:* Levinas uses this term in its etymological sense of the function of a servant. See *En découvrant*, pp. 194–197.]

3. [*Translator's note:* Levinas is playing on two senses of the French verb *signifier*, which means (usually) "to mean," but also "to command."]

4. See on this question pp. 51–55 of my *Noms propres* (Montpellier: Fata Morgana, 1976). I refer the reader also, for a discussion of the problem raised by these Notes on Buber, to Stephane Strasser's beautiful study, "Buber und Levinas, Philosophische Besinnung auf einen Gegensatz," in *Revue internationale de la Philosophie*, 1978, pp. 512–525.

4 Franz Rosenzweig: A Modern Jewish Thinker

1. See Jacob Fleishmann, *The Problems of Christianity in Jewish Thought from Mendelsson to Rosenzweig* ([in Hebrew] Edition Magnès of the Hebrew University of Jerusalem). A remarkably well-informed and intelligent work, sure of its Hegelian orthodoxy, but unperturbed by any doubts.

2. *The Star of Redemption*, trans. W. W. Hallo (Notre Dame: Notre Dame Press, 1970), part 2, pp. 91–111.

3. See Alphonse de Waelhens, *La philosophie de les expériences naturelles* (The Hague: Martinus Nijhoff, 1961) and Jean Hyppolite, *Leçon inaugurale au Collège de France, Faite le jeudi, 19 décembre 1963* (Nogent-le-Rotrou: Imp. Daupeley-Gouverneur, 1964).

4. *The Star of Redemption*, part 1, p. 11.

5. See, for example,Tractate Berachoth, p. 8a.

6. Zionism has changed all that! Rosenzweig is unaware of the significance that a Jewish state assumes for many Jews who have no illusions about nationalism and do not want the Jewish state to be like the others, and who are witnessing the emergence of that state just after the Hitlerian extermination.

7. [*Translator's note:* i.e. Christianity.]

8. Things of the greatest profundity were said on this subject in an old–but not outdated–account by Professor Sholem in 1931 on the occasion of the second edition of *The Star of Redemption*; reprinted in *Judaica*, vol. 106 (Frankfurt: Bibliothek Suhrkamp, 1963), pp. 226–233.

9. See the magnificent pages that Mrs. Eliane Amado Lévy-Valensi has devoted to this theme in *Les Niveaux de l'Être, la Connaissance et le Mal* (Paris: Presses Universitaires de France, 1962), esp. pp. 570–587.

5 Jean Wahl: Neither Having nor Being

1. *Poésie, pensée, perception* (Paris: Calmann Lévy, 1948), p. 26. Henceforth cited as PPP.

2. *L'expérience métaphysique* (Paris: Flammarion, 1965), pp. 20–21. Henceforth cited as EM.

3. *Etudes kierkegaardiennes* (Paris: F. Aubier, 1938), p. 323. Henceforth cited as EK.

4. EK, p. 329.

5. EM, p. 224.

6. PPP, p. 245.

7. *Traité de métaphysique* (Paris: Payot, 1953), p. 703. Henceforth cited as TM.

8. EM, p. 227.

9. TM, p. 703.

10. EM, p. 10.

11. PPP, p. 287.

12. EM, p. 221.

13. TM, p. 721.

14. EM, pp. 8–9.

15. EM, p. 233.

16. EM, p. 232.

17. *Existence humaine et transcendence* (Neuchâtel: n.p., 1944), pp. 35–36. Henceforth cited as EHT.

18. EM, p. 221.

19. EM, p. 132.

20. TM, p. 702.

21. EM, p. 227.

22. EM, p. 223.

23. PPP, p. 18.

24. EM, p. 220.

25. EM, p. 225.

26. EM, pp. 221–222.

27. EM, p. 232.

28. EM, pp. 12–13.

29. PPP, p. 252.

30. TM, p. 702.

31. TM, p. 716.

32. PPP, p. 248.

33. Ibid.
34. PPP, p. 136.
35. EHT, p. 113.
36. PPP, p. 250.
37. TM, p. 721.
38. PPP, p. 25.
39. [*Translator's note:* i.e. *L'expérience métaphysique.*]

7 The Meaning of Meaning

1. [*Translator's note:* i.e. the existential status of that *beyond.*]
2. [*Translator's note:* "Mon semblable, mon frère." These are the concluding words of Baudelaire's well-known introductory poem ("To the Reader") in *The Flowers of Evil.*]
3. [*Translator's note:* "Appraesentation" (German "*Appräsentation*") is an important Husserlian term. It is "the indirect perceptual presentation of an object mediated through the direct presentation of another, e.g., of the rear through the frontal aspect, or of other minds through their minds." (H. Spiegelberg, *The Phenomenological Movement* [The Hague: Martinus Nijhoff, 2nd. ed., 1971], vol. 2, p. 712.)]

8 On Intersubjectivity: Notes on Merleau-Ponty

1. See, in Merleau-Ponty's *Signs* (Evanston: Northwestern University Press, 1964), pp. 159–81, the study entitled "The Philosopher and His Shadow." [*Translator's note:* This work will henceforth be cited as S. I have modified McCleary's translations slightly.]
2. S, p. 166.
3. S, p. 167.
4. Ibid.
5. S, p. 168.
6. Ibid.
7. S, p. 201.
8. [*Translator's note:* On "appresentation," see above, "The Meaning of Meaning," note 3.]
9. S, p. 163.
10. [*Translator's note:* See above, "Apropos of Buber: Some Notes," note 3.]

9 In Memory of Alphonse de Waelhens

1. [*Translator's note:* See above, "On Intersubjectivity: Notes on Merleau-Ponty," note 1.]

2. *Ideen II* (Husserliana, vol. 4).

3. In paragraph 58 and in a note to paragraph 51 of *Ideen I*, Husserl envisages a transcendence of God that would not block the idealist project. [*Translator's note:* In English, see *Ideas Pertaining to a Pure Phenomenology and to a Phenomenological Philosophy*, book 1 (The Hague: Martinus Nijhoff, 1982), pp. 133–134, and 116–117.] That possibility is described in a negative fashion. It would be of interest to determine how that view is concretized in Husserl's unpublished manuscripts.

4. *Ideen I* (Husserliana, vol. 3), p. 103. [*Translator's note:* In English, see Husserl's *Ideas Pertaining*, book 1, p. 125.]

5. Merleau-Ponty, *Signs* (Evanston: Northwestern University Press, 1964), p. 166. Henceforth cited as S.

6. S, p. 159.

7. S, p. 163.

8. On the ambiguity of sensation and sentiment, see my *Otherwise than Being or Beyond Essence*, chapter 2: "Intentionality and Sensing." On the *enigmatic*, see my essay, "Enigme et phénomène," in *En découvrant l'existence avec Husserl et Heidegger*. [*Translator's note:* In English, see "Phenomenon and Enigma," in *Collected Philosophical Papers*, trans. A. Lingis (Dordrecht: Martinus Nijhoff, 1987), pp. 61–73.]

9. [*Translator's note:* On "appresentation," see above, "The Meaning of Meaning," note 3.]

10 The Rights of Man and the Rights of the Other

1. Babylonian Talmud, Tractate Sanhedrin, p. 37a.

2. *Shalom*–peace and benediction–in Hebrew, which resonates, in Psalm 120: 7, as a way for man to refer to himself: "I peace . . ."

3. [*Translator's note:* In French, "*l'autre me regarde*" means both "the other *looks at* me" and "the other *concerns* me." While both senses are "intended" in the passage, it is in the latter sense that the other is, for me, "visage," or face; and it is this latter sense, normally considered the more "figurative," that Levinas makes primary.]

12 Everyday Language and Rhetoric without Eloquence

1. [*Translator's note:* The French "*appariteur*" is the employee of a university who readies the amphitheater and sees to the maintenance of order before and during instruction. The English "attendant" does not convey the etymological connection with the verb "to appear" (Latin "*apparere*") which makes Levinas's metaphor apposite.]

13 The Transcendence of Words: On Michel Leiris's *Biffures*

1. This piece is a critical appraisal of Leiris's *Biffures* (Paris: Gallimard, 1948). [*Translator's note:* See Seán Hand's informative introductory note to this piece in *The Levinas Reader* (Oxford: Blackwell, 1989), pp. 144–145.]

2. [*Translator's note:* Arthur Rimbaud's famous "Sonnet des voyelles" associates the vowel sounds with colors, which are then further developed into a surrealist cornucopia of synesthetic imagery.]

3. Perhaps the expression was suggested by Rabelais' "frozen words," in *Le Quart Livre*, chapter 56.

4. [*Translator's note:* French: "Ce qui se conçoit bien . . . ." A fragment of a well-known verse by Boileau (in *L'Art poétique*, chant I) to the effect that what is well conceived can be stated clearly and easily–a tenet of the poetics of French classicism.]

14 Outside the Subject

1. [*Translator's note:* This rather cryptic formulation appears to define "naive thought" according to Husserl. It would be a thought unaware of what may be posited "otherwise than by thinking," i.e. by affectivity and will, and prone to becoming overly absorbed in the "object," to the point of believing itself to be merely reading off meanings from a "reality" existing independently of its own subjectivity.]

2. E. Husserl, *Ideas Pertaining to a Pure Phenomenology and to a Phenomenological Philosophy,* book 1 (The Hague: Martinus Nijhoff, 1982), p. 191.

3. Ibid.

4. Ibid., p. 301.

Index

Akiba, 130
Anti-Semitism, 62
Appresentation, 93, 100, 112, 114, 115
Aristotle, 135, 139, 151
Augustine, 58, 89, 92
Autarkia, 22

Bachelard, Gaston, 15
Being and Time, 105
Bergson, Henri, 10, 25, 33, 68, 86, 87, 146
Beyond being, 19, 36
Bible, 11, 13, 16, 18, 91, 127–31; Book, the, 126, 129; Old Testament, 123, 128, 130
Biran, Maine de, 19
Blin, Georges, 79
Breda, Herman van, 105
Breton, André, 144
Buber, Martin, 2–47 *passim*, 131

Cartesian Meditations, 112
Castelli, Enrico, 105
Céline, Louis-Ferdinand, 139
Christianity, 51, 52, 59–63, 65
Cogito, 25, 30, 41, 76, 98, 108, 157
Conatus essendi, 3, 43, 48, 92
Creation, 56, 57
Critique of Practical Reason, 157

Critique of Pure Reason, 156
Dasein, 48
David, King, 133
Dead Sea Scrolls, 8
Death, 44, 115
Descartes, 60, 76, 98, 108, 157
De Waelhens, Alphonse, *see* Waelhens, Alphonse de
Diacony, 44
Dialogue, 15, 16, 18, 24–7, 29, 30, 32–4, 36, 39–41, 45, 46, 77, 91, 130, 132
Dis-inter-estment, 36, 47, 87, 115, 124
Dostoyevsky, 44

Ecumenicalism, 52
Egypt, 129
Epochē, 37, 39
Eschatology, 54
Etudes Kierkegaardiennes, 72

Face, 35, 39, 44, 47, 94, 102, 103, 124, 133, 158; face-to-face, 34, 158; feminine, 46
Faith, 3, 81, 90, 93, 115
Feuerbach, Ludwig A., 17
Fleg, Edmond, 11
Freud, Sigmund, 144
Fürsorge, 18

Goethe, 52

169

MERIDIAN

Crossing Aesthetics